LECTIN FREE RECIPE

Easy and Delicious Lectin Free Recipes

(Quick, Easy & Delicious Lectin Free Crock Pot Recipes)

Christy Stewart

Published by Alex Howard

© **Christy Stewart**

All Rights Reserved

Lectin Free Recipe: Easy and Delicious Lectin Free Recipes (Quick, Easy & Delicious Lectin Free Crock Pot Recipes)

ISBN 978-1-990169-17-5

All rights reserved. No part of this guide may be reproduced in any form without permission in writing from the publisher except in the case of brief quotations embodied in critical articles or reviews.

Legal & Disclaimer

The information contained in this book is not designed to replace or take the place of any form of medicine or professional medical advice. The information in this book has been provided for educational and entertainment purposes only.

The information contained in this book has been compiled from sources deemed reliable, and it is accurate to the best of the Author's knowledge; however, the Author cannot guarantee its accuracy and validity and cannot be held liable for any errors or omissions. Changes are periodically made to this book. You must consult your doctor or get professional medical advice before using any of the suggested remedies, techniques, or information in this book.

Table of contents

- PART 1 1
- INTRODUCTION 2
- CHAPTER 1: WHAT ARE LECTINS? 4
- CHAPTER 2: THE PLANT PARADOX 9
  - The Author 9
  - The Response 11
  - A Meaningful Conversation 13
- CHAPTER 3: UNDERSTANDING PLANT LECTINS 15
- CHAPTER 4: HOW LECTINS CAUSE DIGESTIVE PROBLEMS 17
- CHAPTER 5: LECTINS, INFLAMMATION, & IMMUNE DEFICIENCY ... 20
- CHAPTER 6: LECTINS' INTERFERENCE IN CELLULAR FUNCTIONING ... 25
- CHAPTER 7: WGA'S INFLUENCE ON BLOOD SUGAR & FAT CELLS ... 27
- CHAPTER 8: LECTIN SENSITIVITY 30
- CHAPTER 9: BENEFITS OF A LECTIN-FREE DIET 32
- CHAPTER 10: GETTING STARTED WITH A LECTIN-FREE DIET ... 36
- CHAPTER 11: WHAT TO EAT AND AVOID WHILE FOLLOWING A LECTIN-FREE DIET 46
- CHAPTER 12: SUCCESS WITH THE LECTIN-FREE DIET 55
  - The Expensive Side Of The Plant Paradox Diet 57
- CHAPTER 13: AN EVALUATION OF THE LECTIN-FREE DIET 60
  - The Facts And True Theory About Lectins 63
- CHAPTER 14: BENEFITS OF LECTINS 65
- CHAPTER 15: RISKS OF A LECTIN-FREE DIET 68
  - A Lectin-Free Diet? 68
  - Plant-Based Diet And Lectin Quantity 70

DISADVANTAGES OF A LECTIN-FREE DIET 71
LECTIN AS ANTINUTRIENT 72

CHAPTER 16: MYTHS ABOUT LECTINS 73

THE CONTROVERSIAL DIET 74
THEORIES AROUND LECTINS 77
INFORMATION ABOUT LECTINS 77
COMMON FOOD TOXINS 78
SELENIUM POISONING 79
MERCURY POISONING 79
AMYLASE INHIBITORS 79
ANTI-THIAMINE COMPOUNDS 80

CHAPTER 17: AN ALTERNATIVE TO A LECTIN-FREE DIET 81

CHAPTER 18: WHAT IS THE ULTIMATE NUTRITION-BASED DIET PLAN? 89

REASONS TO STICK TO A DIET PLAN 89
GOOD NUTRITION 90
PORTION-CONTROL DIET 91
PORTIONWISE NUTRITION CONTENT 92
LECTINS (THE PLANT PARADOX) 93
THE OVERALL BEST DIET FOR A PERSON 94
CONCERNS REGARDING LECTINS IN DIETS 95

CONCLUSION 98

PART 2 100

VEGETARIAN RECIPES 107

CREAMY CAULIFLOWER MASHED 107
TASTY HERBED MUSHROOMS 109
EASY BRUSSELS SPROUTS 111
SIMPLE DIJON BRUSSELS SPROUTS 112
GARLIC KALE 113
HEALTHY SLOW COOKER SPINACH 114
EASY LEMON GARLIC ASPARAGUS 116
WARM MILLET 118
CAULIFLOWER COCONUT CURRY 119

Lemon Thyme Carrots 120
Lemon Artichokes 122
Creamy Sweet Potato Mashed 124
Delicious Root Vegetables 125
Mushroom Stroganoff 127
Healthy Roasted Vegetables 128
Savory Sweet Potato Mash 129
Parsnips Cauliflower Mash 131
Roasted Herb Beets 133
Herbed Onion Mushrooms 134
Simple Collard Greens 135

SOUP & STEW RECIPES 136

Creamy Broccoli Cauliflower Soup 136
Perfect Cauliflower Soup 138
Healthy Ginger Broccoli Soup 139
Delicious Beef Chili 141
Creamy Mushroom Soup 143
Beef Cabbage Soup 145
Chicken Cabbage Soup 147
Okra Beef Stew 149
Creamy Asparagus Soup 151
Mushroom Asparagus Soup 152
Leek Sweet Potato Soup 153
Salmon Coconut Stew 154
Chicken Mushroom Soup 155
Easy Carrot Soup 157
Creamy Carrot Sweet Potato Soup 159
Simple Chicken Vegetable Soup 161
Avocado Chicken Soup 163
Healthy Spinach Broccoli Soup 165
Creamy Garlic Asparagus Soup 166
Cauliflower Asparagus Soup 168

MEAT RECIPES 170

Pork With Cabbage 170

- Chicken With Garlicky Spinach 172
- Artichoke Spinach Chicken 174
- Beef Chuck Roast 176
- Roasted Pork Shoulder 178
- Delicious Pork Chops 179
- Healthy Lemon Dill Halibut 181
- Salmon With Carrots & Onions 183
- Cilantro Lime Salmon 185
- Chicken With Artichokes 186
- Delicious Turkey With Gravy 188
- Delicious Beef With Mushrooms 190

Part 1

Introduction

Dieting has become more versatile with the introduction of many diet programs. Yet, selecting a reliable diet program isn't easy. You have to do your homework before settling on any particular program. Seldom do people spend enough time doing the homework before deciding on a diet plan. This is the main reason why diet fads have become common. It's also the reason why so many people try diets, have limited success, and then abandon the strategy. If you are trying to lose weight, you must have an understanding of the foods that make you gain weight. It's high time to find the issues.

Are you having problems with digestion? Or are you struggling with unexplained bloating? Has inflammation taken a toll on your immune system? Then, you need to learn about the lectin-free diet!

Once you understand the lectin-free diet, you can decide whether to follow it or not. I'm not going to be biased.

You might have wasted a lot of effort to lose weight, but then, lectins come into the picture and spoil everything. But the problem is that many people do not know the issues with lectins. Plant-based foods such as beans, nuts, whole grains, and much more can cause inflammation, and they can become a barrier in your weight-loss journey. Did you know that? I also did not know this until I started researching it.

Specific studies have been done by many successful people on the lectin-free diet. And those projects have helped millions of dieters. You don't have to consume tedious items anymore. You can live a healthy life.

If you consider the statistics, you will find that a lot of people have witnessed positive changes once they opted for a lectin-free diet. They have set themselves free from inflammation and immune issues. What more could you ask for? But, wait! There's a lot to know about a lectin-free diet. So, keep reading!

You don't have to restrain yourself from eating delicious dishes because you can find a lot of lectin-free recipes online. It is not going to be hard, and you will not find obstacles in your journey to follow the lectin-free diet.

You don't have to damage your health anymore. Once you understand the lectin-free diet in detail, you will be able to clearly know the things that have been confusing you for so long. After you get a grip on this diet, you can maintain your body without facing any issues such as inflammation or immune problems.

If you are confused about what a lectin-free diet is or whether it is good or bad, this book could help you understand the pros and cons of a lectin-free diet. Once you read this book, you should have a crystal-clear view of this diet, and you can make an informed decision. You don't have to make use of guesswork or face any confusion because this book will include everything that you need to know as a beginner.

First, we'll lay out what lectins are before considering several ways that they do damage within the human body.

Education plays an important role when you try to adopt or change something. Especially when it comes to a particular diet, you must make sure to learn it before you adopt it! You must get a grip on the foods that you can or cannot eat. You must know how lectins harm your body. If you don't make an effort, you will never understand what a lectin-free diet is!

There are a lot of things to be learned, so let's get started!

Chapter 1: What Are Lectins?

What are lectins? These are proteins that stick to cell membranes. They cause issues to the immune system while disrupting cell interaction. You will find lectins in grains, vegetables, dairy products, and raw legumes. Also, they are abundant in seeds and seed coats.

Most people weren't aware of lectins until recently. These erythrocyte-agglutinating proteins have been in the picture since the 19th century. (Agglutinate is just a fancy word for "stick together," since lectins have a tendency to stick to things.) In the 1960s, it was evident that these proteins agglutinate sugar-specific proteins, too. Lectins are common in plants and seldom seen naturally in vertebrates. Peter Hermann Stillmark, a microbiologist, was the person who originated the definition of lectins. His doctoral thesis was done on the toxic lectin in castor beans. Over time, scientists started researching lectins and came to understand them in greater detail. As understanding grew, health professionals began focusing more on lectins and their effects on human health.

However, before the 1970s, only a few lectins gained attention. Slowly, other lectins were identified as useful while others were understood as harmful to humans. Later, additional lectins were discovered in animals, microorganisms, plants, and humans, with ongoing revelations about their impacts.

When lectins are found in common carbohydrates like legumes and grains, they form glycoproteins. Glycoproteins support the immune system and keep protein levels under control. Yet, as the saying goes, "too much of anything is good for nothing," you must not consume too many lectins. If you do, they will create adverse effects on your health. You will have problems such as diarrhea, vomiting, and much more. These changes are caused due to issues in immune functions.

Concurrently, you might have heard lectins hold a special place in supporting the body functions and health. So, what about those? Well, there are specific lectins which are essential to your body. These lectins create positive reactions in the human body. They prevent certain diseases. Plus, your body needs lectins to perform certain functions.

Yet the reason we have written this book is because much (virtual) ink has been spilled in recent years stating that lectins generally have a negative impact upon human health. So this is high time to learn about lectins and what we understand about their positive and negative impacts. You must learn why and how lectins are making you unhealthy, if they truly are doing so. Let's begin by learning a few basic ways in which they affect your health.

Lectins will not be digested because people produce antibodies to support them. We all have antibodies in our bodies for specific dietary lectins. However, different people respond differently to dietary lectins. Some foods can be intolerable for some people due to changes in their immune systems, among other reasons. Specific lectins have the power to stimulate the immune system very quickly. And there are some particular lectins that should be avoided altogether.

For example, raw red kidney beans should be wholly avoided due to the lectin phytohaemagglutinin they contain. It makes raw kidney beans poisonous. Once 4-5 beans are swallowed, the symptoms will start to show. Kidney beans contain 20,000-70,000 lectin units when they are raw and 200-400 when they are completely cooked. Consuming phytohaemagglutinin can increase intestinal gas, a phenomenon most of us are all too familiar with after consuming beans. In large quantities, this lectin may result in vomiting and diarrhea.

Lectins are very tricky to avoid on a daily basis. If you suspect that foods containing lectins are causing your health problems, then one easy way to find out is to stay away from packaged goods that contain lectins. You have to pay attention because manufacturers of processed and prepared foods can sneak lectins into foods without being obvious, like a corn-based sweetener or a soy-based dressing.

Yet this principle about packaged and processed food does not mean that the opposite is true. Many whole, raw plant-based foods are the worst offenders when it comes to the impacts of lectins. For instance, it's common knowledge that unrefined (whole) grains are more nutritious than refined grains. Yet, you will find more lectins in unrefined grains. So, what's better— whole grains or refined grains? The answer may not be the same for all people.

Whole grains were not an issue in the past when people harvested and worked on their own grains. But, now, people have quick access to processed grains, and they consume too much of them. In the broad scope of humanity's gene pool and the granular view of each individual's tolerance, our bodies are not adequately equipped for consumption of the lectins that whole grains contain. Even if our ancient ancestors were so equipped, that doesn't mean we will be. That's the reason why things such as legumes, dairy, cereals, soybeans, and peanuts are related to digestive problems. Seafood also contains a higher level of lectins.

Some people are allergic to lectins. In that case, they might react immediately, so it is better for them to avoid lectins completely. Some carry this allergy genetically whereas some others develop it over time.

Pro tip: If you want to check whether you are sensitive to lectins, try eliminating them from your diet. And then, add them slowly to your diet again, and check for symptoms.

However, there are some benefits to consuming certain foods that contain lectins. Ultimately, you have to decide what's right and what's not by considering the pros and cons. But knowing the pros and cons of the diet will not suffice. You must also observe the impacts of lectin-rich foods, whether you are allergic to lectins, and the overall condition of your health. Either way, the age-old wisdom still stands: it is much better to consume foods moderately. What moderation looks like for you or whether it is possible are individual choices. But in order to make that choice, you need the complete picture of the lectin-free diet. Let's get a deep dive into the topic.

Gastrointestinal distress occurs due to damages caused by lectins to the intestinal lining. When food enters the gut, there will be minor damages to the lining of the tract. Usually, this damage will be repaired in a short time. The gut lining can take care of itself, so it is crucial for the repair system to be completely efficient. Still, lectins will feint the quick recovery procedure. Your cells will lose the ability to regenerate as they did beforehand, due to the damage caused by lectins. Thus, gut defenses will be compromised, and the lining will become leaky, letting in unwanted molecules. Your body will be unable to absorb minerals and vitamins in the right way. Once you consume too many lectins, they will damage your GI tract and cause cramping, vomiting, and diarrhea. The effect is similar to drinking too much alcohol.

With the damages caused to the GI tract, there will be complications for the immune system's response, as well. You will witness symptoms such as joint pain, skin rashes, and inflammation.

If you have diseases such as irritable bowel syndrome or Crohn's disease, foods with lectins may make these conditions worse because of the irritation to your gut lining. This can be due to a higher number of immature cells, and they have the space to attract lectins. You will suffer until the dietary lectins leave the body. But, you can quicken the voiding process by eating vegetables, fruits, and other foods that can fight against lectins.

Before we move on, do you think everyone should eliminate lectins? It is a controversial issue. For some people, it is better to avoid lectins completely. On the other hand, some might not have noticeable issues with lectins. If you have irritable bowel syndrome or autoimmune conditions, it is better to avoid lectin-containing food so that you don't have

Chapter 2: The Plant Paradox

Even as mankind's discovery of lectins has been fairly recent, and our understanding is still rather shallow, so the concept of a lectin-based diet is a recent phenomenon. Only time with tell whether it should be rightly characterized as a fad versus a viable and preferable nutritional philosophy.

The Author

One man is responsible for bringing into the mainstream the theory of lectins' harm to the human body: Dr. Steven Gundry. In his own words (presumably)[1], Dr. Gundry has had a career of over 30 years "as one of the world's pre-eminent experts in heart surgery." In fact, he and his former partner Leonard Bailey are said to have performed more infant and pediatric heart transplants than any other surgeons in the world after they developed the preferred technique for doing so.[2]

Yet his expertise extends beyond those mere pedestrian achievements. He has also influenced or originated several various technological advances and other surgical procedures within the medical field. He holds several patents and is credited with developing truly meaningful and deployable procedures that have made the healthcare profession more effective.

His reputation and prestige are second to none, with a history of the finest training, election to prestigious fellowships and influential societies, and membership on boards of leadership in the medical field. One factor that sets him apart from his peers is his self-proclaimed love of research, which led him to write more papers than any of his predecessors in the residency program at the University of Michigan. His quest for knowledge and breakthroughs seems to be a constant theme in his career.

By all measurements, he has been a well respected and impactful member of the medical profession.

Despite those successes, it seems that the hallmark of Dr. Gundry's career had its origin in 2001, when he began to work with an overweight patient who had been shunted away by other physicians as a "hopeless case"[3]. "With nothing but a combination of natural, dietary nutrients," this individual made an astounding turnaround and changed his dire prognosis. It was a watershed moment for Dr. Gundry, when he realized that he didn't wish to continue repairing the effects of chronic disease but would rather prevent it to begin with.

In 2008, Dr. Gundry published his first book, entitled Dr. Gundry's Diet Evolution: Turn Off the Genes That Are Killing You and Your Waistline. As the title indicates, the book's fundamental focus and seemingly the core of his philosophy at that time was the genetic basis for human disease. The prescriptions for addressing disease and poor health look similar to what he had learned years before—nutrition and diet.

Dr. Gundry's nutritional and dietetic expertise shows up prominently once again in 2016, as the singer-turned-actor Usher used Gundry's "Matrix diet" to transform his body shape. Doing so took him from his characteristic long and slender look to the thick and muscular body type of the boxer Sugar Ray Leonard, whom Usher played in the movie Hands of Stone.[4] The Matrix diet consists of a dual strategy wherein meals are consumed with greater frequency—six times a day instead of three—and there is some intentionality about the types of foods that are eaten. Usher also worked out three times each day in a variety of workout types.

When one looks at the business Dr. Gundry runs from his website today, it appears that his interest is more broad and comprehensive than the issue of lectins. He offers supplements that seem to be proprietary blends of naturally occurring substances—nothing basic like iron or calcium. Costs range from

$24.95 on the low end for a bottle of Vitamin D 5000 to $240 for the TriTrim weight management product.

His other major product line features skincare products that offer a means to deliver vital bodily nutrition directly through the body's highly permeable covering, the skin. Costs here begin at $65 for a Gentle Botanical Cleanser. The high end includes several products listed at $120. (He is based in California, after all.)

Lastly, Gundry MD also features some boutique food products with enhanced features. $15.95 can secure a pouch of freeze-dried Spring Medley snack mix. For $54.95, you can enjoy some Polyphenol Pearls, what appear to be olive oil capsules.

While he offers these products in keeping with his mission "To dramatically improve human health, happiness, and longevity through (his) unique vision of diet and nutrition," his overriding understanding about what makes for human health starts with the gut and the beneficial microbes that dwell and function there.

The Response

What really brought Dr. Gundry and his controversial convictions into the broad public eye was his 2017 book, The Plant Paradox: Hidden Dangers in "Healthy" Foods That Cause Disease and Weight Gain. Here he makes his case against lectins, citing disease and weight gain as their primary negative consequences. He suggests that this book and its complementary volume, The Plant Paradox Cookbook, are his "proudest achievements"[5].

Much of the content reflected in The Plant Paradox will be covered within this book, though it's worth noting that Gundry's book is a must-read if you intend to begin a lectin-free diet. One of the book's highlights is its three-phase process to begin and continue with a lectin-free lifestyle. In those phases, he tells you how to start off with a cleanse that sets the body's baseline for the drastic change it will encounter on the lectin-free diet. Then as you follow the diet, your body begins to repair itself and restore the body to its highest level of health. Finally, having faithfully followed a lectin-free diet, you will reap rewards that the book describes in the third and interminable phase.

Upon its release, The Plant Paradox debuted at #2 on its respective New York Times bestseller list and remained there for a respectable 19 weeks. Immediately, a natural connection was established between lectins and the previously vilified plant protein gluten. Common sentiment seemed to embrace the obvious danger of lectins based upon the demonstrable harm that gluten caused for many people. The Atlantic warned "Lectins Could Become the Next Gluten."[6]

The irony of the association between gluten and lectins is that Dr. Gundry himself argues that gluten-free foods are part of the problem with poor health.[7] But it's not for the reason you might suspect. His point is that people consume more lectins eating gluten-free or substitute foods, and while gluten is problematic, these other lectins and their quantities are a far graver ill.

Dr. Gundry's book drew the interest of all sorts of publications, ranging from Psychology Today to Huff Post and US News. Of course, the "deviant health trends" genre of websites latched on to the concept lustily, with plenty of intellectual food for consumption.

While the enthusiasm and vigor that first accompanied the book's release has waned in the mainstream, it still garners considerable attention—both positive and negative—as a diet and nutritional plan to be reckoned with. It is too compelling to ignore.

And new life was breathed into the idea in the middle of 2018 when American Idol winner Kelly Clarkson went public with her great success on the diet. That eye-catching information attracted the attention of People, Good Housekeeping, Family

Circle, and Cooking Light. It also provided extra buzz at the time of the release of The Plant Paradox Cookbook.

Not all of the responses have been flattering. One particularly whimsical rejoinder proposes "The Oxygen Paradox," whereby we entirely eliminate oxygen from human consumption.[8] In fact, a popular method of response is to play off of the word "paradox," with variations for poultry and observations that there is a paradox in that the plan doesn't follow scientific protocols for weight loss.

The critical responses often contain a level of snark and condescension that leads one to wonder about motivations. It's no secret that doctors have egos, and one wonders if personal pride fuels some of the tone, if not perhaps the conclusions.

In May 2019, a simple Google search for "The Plant Paradox" returns 37,800,000 results, and not all of them are connected to Dr. Gundry's savvy offshoot marketing. The scale is nowhere near the same, but you can still find 941,000 hits for the search term "Steven Gundry." It seems that he's doing pretty well for himself.

A Meaningful Conversation

The conversation is important. If the claims of the lectin-free diet are true, then the rewards are so great as to make almost any sacrifice or lifestyle change worthwhile. On the other hand, the food restrictions of the lectin-free diet are so extensive and contrary to traditional notions of healthy nutrition that if the conclusions about the diet are not true, then following the diet would be the height of foolishness.

These questions are perhaps more difficult to clarify than ever before in humanity's quest for knowledge and understanding. As one set of commentators expressed, the phenomenon of "fake news" has become a bane to humanity's ability to function and interrelate, and pop culture nutrition information has not avoided the trend. They warn that "The proliferation of fabricated 'facts' and ignored truths are a great menace to our society"[9]. So it is a noble quest that you have pursued to get to the bottom of whether the lectin-free diet has merit, particularly for your unique situation and circumstances.

Some fundamental questions that you will need to resolve include:

- Is Dr. Gundry credible?
- Is Dr. Gundry trustworthy?
- Are there other trusted authorities who agree with Dr. Gundry's conclusions? How many?
- Is the research sound?
- Is there real-life evidence showing the success of the lectin-free diet in the lives of relatively normal people?
- Is there bias present in any of the information—either for or against the lectin-free diet?
- Are there hidden agendas that could be motivating either side?
- What is at stake if I am wrong?

The goal of this book is to provide as much objective, factual information as possible to aid you in formulating answers to these questions. While we may express an opinion in interpretation of factual information, we will not attempt to sway your decision. People are not created as carbon copies of one another, and we feel that each individual must make informed decisions about what is best for his or her health. So we wish to provide you with power—through information—and freedom to make your own decision.

With those thoughts in mind, let's turn now to the plant paradox itself—the lectins that are of the greatest concern, those that are found within plants.

Chapter 3: Understanding Plant Lectins

The term "lectin" is undoubtedly new to many people. While these proteins are gaining mainstream attention, it's important to remain cautious about drawing hasty conclusions. Even our most confidently held scientific notions can have rather thin bases undergirding them. The checkered history of conclusions about the health of butter versus margarine is a cautionary tale. Though we have a basic understanding about what lectins are, where they are found, and how they function in the human body, there is still much to learn. Research into lectins continues. So, it is no wonder people have thousands of questions about lectins. But, the molecular world cannot be studied or understood that quickly. It is a fantastic world. Its intricacy and detail require a methodical and painstaking approach for its study.

Generally, you can find twenty-five classifications of lectins. Those are the ones that have been researched so far. In a lectin-free diet, your concern will be about the plant lectins. These plant lectins can be found in soybeans, peanuts, corn, beans, peppers, potatoes, tomatoes, and in some plant grains. As you can see, there are some common and enjoyable food items at stake in this issue. Let's get started!

In 1888, Peter Hermann Stillmark found plant lectins. The research was done by extracting protein from castor bean seeds in order to observe how it binds to the red blood cells in animals. The same research was carried out on other plant seeds, too. The high level of proteins contained in legumes made it easy for the scientists to characterize the seeds based on the results.

Through the research, it was found that plant lectins fall under the category of glycan-binding proteins. These proteins stick to carbohydrates in your bloodstream. In plants, the lectins provide energy for the plant in its period of early growth, and then the lectins disappear. Taking advantage of this principle, stimulating the sprouting of seeds and nuts before consuming them is useful because it reduces plant lectins.

Another function of lectins within their plants is to act as a defense tool. It is impossible for plants to fight against animals, so the lectins protect them against invaders that will damage or kill the plant. For instance, when an insect eats a plant, it ingests the lectins in the plant. Those lectins bind to the cells in the insect's body. Slowly, the immune system and the endocrine system of the insect will be altered due to the plant lectins. So, the issue here is whether the plant can differentiate animals and humans? Clearly, the plant cannot. The harmful effects seen in insects and animals will be the same for humans.

But, the great news is humans have natural defense techniques that protect us against unnoticed threats. The microbiome in the human body fights against microbes, helps to break down foods, provides instructions to the immune system, and also produces vitamins for your body. The human defense tools, include the barrier to absorption provided by the lining of the intestines, the immune system, saliva, and much more that keep us alive. So, if you have consumed plant lectins, your body's natural defense techniques have protected them from harming you.

This is the ideal scenario. But when we consider modern health statistics, it seems that the average person's health is anything but ideal. So what are the problems? And are they rightly attributed to lectins? We will consider these questions in the next chapter.

Chapter 4: How Lectins Cause Digestive Problems

The health dangers caused by lectins can be insidious. For people who are basically healthy, the extent of lectin-based dysfunction in the human body is directly related to the concentration of lectins consumed. So someone who consumes a relatively low amount of lectins could have a range of minor ailments or conditions that she has become accustomed to suffering without thinking twice about the cause—let alone suspecting that it could be due to lectins. At the same time, the major health issues that can arise from a diet heavily saturated with lectins can be so varied that one might never attribute them to something consumed on a regular basis.

For these reasons, it is important that you understand the basic ways that harmful lectins cause disruption in the human body. Likewise, there is great value in understanding how those basic activities can cause unique problems in a variety of bodily systems. By studying this information, you will be equipped to recognize the symptoms of lectin-based disease in yourself and others.

The fundamental aspect of lectins that starts the chain-reaction of distress is that they are "sticky proteins" and readily bond to sugar-based substances like glycoproteins, glycolipids, and carbohydrates. These sugar-based substances tend to stick to cell membranes, so when they have lectins attached to them, then those lectins are in close proximity to healthy cells. When lectins stick to the intestinal wall, or epithelium, and remain there for some time, it causes problems. The lectins cause irritation, and the intestinal lining becomes inflamed. The digestive tract's epithelial cells may begin to die, and their rate of regeneration can decline. At the same time, the accretion of lectin-bound cells on the intestinal wall limit its surface area and therefore hinders its efficient absorption of the nutrients the body and the intestine itself need. The lack of proper nutrient absorption prevents the intestines from repairing the inflammation caused by lectins, and eventually the intestinal wall becomes abnormally and unhealthily permeable. The name "leaky gut syndrome" is applied to this particular condition. This permeability then allows undigested food particles and many other toxins to enter the bloodstream. At that point, a whole host of additional risks come into play, and we will turn to those momentarily.

The problems taking place in the gut can be subtle enough to be unnoticeable. Perhaps you have more gas than usual, or the odor is stronger. However, as the condition worsens, you are likely to experience nausea, stomach upset, or cramping. Loose bowels, diarrhea, or vomiting can result without intervention. Finally, you may experience blood in your stool or vomit, and this is always an indication of a major problem that requires emergency treatment.

Once the gut wall is damaged, it is not hard for lectins to bypass this essential barrier of protection. Once lectins invade, it will not be hard for them to access the bloodstream, glands, and lymph nodes. The worst part is that even the bacterial and dietary compounds which shouldn't be granted access through the gut wall will be able to enter pretty easily. Then the door opens to widespread risks to the body, as bacteria and other foreign matter are granted free reign to travel throughout the body. When the wall is damaged, there is no other way to protect the body from lectins that are ingested, and the cycle continues. Ultimately, under such a barrage of threats, the body will lose the ability to fight back.

To visualize the process by which the gut comes under threat from lectins, you can compare your gut to the principles and values that guide your life. Let's say you have a certain code of ethics, and you don't accept anything that breaches your ethics. Instead, you only accept the things that adhere to your code of ethics. So, you set boundaries to take in good things and to let go of bad things. In the human digestive system, the intestinal wall acts as a boundary to absorb the good things and release or fend off the bad things. So, when demanding people keep pushing you to accept values or principles that go against your ethical code, you may buckle under the pressure. The chances of giving up on your code of ethics are high because of their persistent and potentially violent assaults. Similarly, lectins are demanding and relentless, and somehow manage to connect to the gut wall despite the body's efforts to resist.

Once you give up on your ethics, there will be huge damage, or you might come to a point where you'd give up all your ethical convictions. Demanding people can induce such drastic compromise. With lectin proteins, it is the same story. Once they stick to the gut wall, they start damaging it while blocking good nutrients from entering the wall. This is the significant harm caused by lectins.

Chapter 5: Lectins, Inflammation, & Immune Deficiency

Even though lectins are dangerous, the human body is a miracle which naturally has the power to fight back against a lot of things, including lectins. The following natural defenses can stop lectins from harming your body.

Saliva. One reason why your mouth has saliva is to snatch away threats like lectins without letting them travel throughout your body. The extra coat of saliva on your tongue and throat protects your body from danger. To have saliva in your mouth, you must drink a lot of water. The most straightforward reason is that, without water, it's impossible to make saliva. If you want to boost your self-defense, make sure to stay hydrated. Thus, when lectins are ingested by your body, they can quickly be flushed out.

Mucus. This is one of the body's leading defense tools against lectins. The human nose has a mucus lining which collects and traps pollutants, foreign matter, and small substances that are harmful to the body. Mucus is present in your intestine, as well. The intestinal mucosal barrier remains as a protective layer to separate lectins from the body and the gut. Thus, it helps to protect the body from lectins.

Gastric Acid. Although most lectins are immune to digestion, specific lectins can be broken down by gastric acid.

Microbiome. Your gut is lined with a microbiome of bacteria that offers natural protection. Even before lectins invade your body's cells, bacteria will destroy them. (Note: Artificial sweeteners, like aspartame and sucralose, will kill bacteria in your gut. In the meantime, the risk of heart attack increases when you consume artificial sweeteners.)

The body has a strong defense mechanism. It will neutralize and wash out everything that doesn't suit your body. As you undoubtedly know well, that process is not particularly enjoyable, though it is necessary and ultimately beneficial.

Despite these powerful natural defense techniques, for many of us, our bodies are not capable of overcoming the presence of lectins. For others, our eating habits provide such a heavy concentration of lectins that our defense mechanisms are overwhelmed and cannot prevail.

When lectins are no longer hindered by a healthy intestinal lining and pass through the gut's epithelial membrane, they are free to run rampant throughout the body, causing havoc on whatever sugar-based molecules they encounter. Likewise, because of the permeability of the epithelium, other matter including undigested food particles and indigestible substances escape into the bloodstream, to be transported and deposited at random throughout the body.

When this happens, white blood cells do their jobs to protect your body. They release IFN-gamma, TNF-alpha, and IL-1. These molecules support inflammation and help to encounter and destroy foreign invaders. The reason that the body executes an inflammatory response is to trap and destroy the foreign matter before it does damage within the body. We tend to view inflammation as a bad thing because it is painful or uncomfortable and limits our ability to function in the ways we would like, but in these types of temporary emergency scenarios, it is highly beneficial and a process that we should allow to run its course unhindered. Yet chronic inflammation is an obvious indication of an undermined organ or body system.

Inflammation throughout the body is perhaps the most commonly cited harm caused by food-based lectins. You may be surprised to know that arthritis isn't caused by a problem in the bones, but by inflammation due to lectins. Yet it is still common to understand arthritis as a bone condition.

Inflammation in the body is an indication that the body is waging an immune response against a perceived threat. So when the epithelial wall of the intestines is inflamed, the immune system is already hard at work. The immune system creates antibodies to work against lectins. The fight to keep foreign objects out of our bloodstream puts stress on the immune system, especially when more fuel is routinely dumped on the fire, so to speak. Leaky gut syndrome creates the occasion for a cornucopia of threats from foreign matter.

You can compare your immune system to a scanner. It checks everything that enters your body. The white blood cells perform this scanning function. If white blood cells identify something as good for the body, they will let it pass. If they recognize it as unhealthy, they will attack it.

But, what if your immune system has weakened or become compromised in its capacity? How long will these defense mechanisms persist? The duration may differ depending upon the individual's body condition. If you don't protect your defenses, those defenses might not be able to protect you.

You can hurt the percentage of bacteria in your body through factors such as antibacterial products, stomach acid blockers, and NSAIDs. Both good and bad bacteria will be reduced from your body. When that happens, the gut's capacity reduces; it will not be able to break down the lectins as it did before. Thus, continuous consumption of high-lectin food can outstrip the power of defenses.

So, when you ingest plant lectins that cannot be handled by bacteria, they get deposited on the gut wall. This is when you start experiencing leaky-gut issues. For instance, when you continuously consume soybeans, the lectins in soybeans will be attracted to carbohydrates in your bloodstream. If your gut barrier is healthy, the small intestine will not let the proteins reach your bloodstream. But, if your gut barrier is not in good condition, the proteins might reach their target.

Sadly, lectins can stick to healthy cells, and thereby limit the immune system's effectiveness. This scenario leaves the immune system in disarray and confusion. Should it attack the foreign invaders, even at the risk of healthy cells? If not, what is the risk of leaving the lectins unmanaged? Our bodies are not prepared to address this confusion. As a result, harmful lectins are allowed to remain in the body to disrupt other bodily systems or they are attacked by the immune system, causing damage to otherwise healthy organs.

There are two main processes whereby the immune system misfires in this way.

Dual Receptors. Some white blood cells consist of bi-scanners. Thus, they utilize the scanners simultaneously. There will be a conflict when one scanner recognizes some substances as good and the other as bad. As studies have shown, dual receptors activate two separate defense mechanisms when a new substance, like a lectin, enters the body. One of the defense mechanisms will fight against lectins, and the other will harm the healthy tissues. Over time, white blood cells will make the immune system damage the healthy tissues whenever lectins enter the body. The autoimmune response becomes natural due to the reactivity of dual receptors. In simple terms, the immune system doesn't decide anything, and the trigger is a new substance, i.e., lectins. This is the reason to consider the lectin-free or a low-lectin diet. If you don't consume lectins, the immune system will not be triggered to react such a way.

Dual Reactivity. When the processes that lectins undergo in the body appear similar to those undergone by bodily tissue, a phenomenon called molecular mimicry occurs. In essence, the immune system becomes confused and treats healthy tissue like a foreign substance because they are both similar. For example, the white blood cell in a person's body may attack a healthy thyroid while the other focuses on lectins. What does this mean? There are higher chances for lectins (the foreign substance) to mimic your healthy tissue.

Understanding plant lectins can be tough because there are still things that are unknown. Scientists are still in the process of understanding how and which lectins cause autoimmune responses. Meanwhile, some people might develop Multiple Sclerosis, Hashimoto's, and many other diseases due to consuming lectins that react negatively in their systems. Furthermore, lectins make it easier for viruses to stick to your cells.

Even if you know that you have consumed lectins regularly, and it seems that they have caused no ill effects to your health, you shouldn't quickly dismiss the possibility that underlying damage is taking place. When you get used to something—how you feel and the way your body functions—you become habituated and no longer perceive a difference. You can become comfortable with and blind to subpar health! We tend to accept it automatically. Unfortunately, you may not be aware of the problems caused by lectins until a problematic condition has advanced to a chronic level.

Chapter 6: Lectins' Interference In Cellular Functioning

Inflammation is one of the more broadly researched and accepted effects of lectins. The way lectins cause inflammation is that first it binds with the carbohydrates that are present in our bodies. One of the side effects of this type of binding is the loss of communication between cells. This disruption in communication leads to inflammatory reactions in the human body. For example, when a neuron tries to send a message to another neuron, the communication can be blocked by lectins. This is what often underlies brain fog. Eventually, you will face a reduction in mental performance.

One of the body's chief mechanisms for cellular communication and coordination is the endocrine system, the array of glands and hormones released by them to provide instructions to various cells and systems in the body. Hormones are essential in the body because they are like the head of a firm who delegates authority. They give instructions to tissues and cells. They keep the body's processes under control and coordinated. Lectins can interfere with hormonal functions because of how endocrine receptors interact with lectins. Lectins can camouflage hormones or even change the messages which might have been sent to tissues and cells. Hence, this endocrine interference will result in negative effects for the body, with the potential to disrupt any system influenced by hormones.

Because of their binding properties, lectins have the power to cluster cells together, a phenomenon called agglutination. When lectins do this, cells become confined and "landlocked" and are not able to function optimally. They lack the necessary surface area on their membranes to permit the vital exchange of materials into and out of the cell. Numerous adverse effects occur. When immune cells are agglutinated by lectins, lectins can eventually gain the power to inactivate them. This leads to autoimmune problems and allergies.

Mitogens are substances that support cell division, or mitosis, by acting as catalysts for that process. There is evidence that lectins' interference on the activity of mitogens may result in cells replicating in a cancerous form. They have been suspected of aiding abnormal growth within vital internal organs.

Lastly, since lectins diminish the digestive system's ability to absorb nutrients, cells can be starved of the essential raw materials and building blocks they require to participate in metabolic processes. These missing nutrients may include lipids, proteins, and carbohydrates.

Chapter 7: Wga's Influence On Blood Sugar & Fat Cells

The lectin Wheat Germ Agglutinin (WGA) is one of the most destructive lectins and a primary reason for the health issues humans face due to lectin consumption. There are implications for its involvement in bringing about chronic diseases like celiac disease and heart disease. WGA is referred to as a cereal grain lectin, and it is most commonly found in wheat germ, wheat-based breakfast cereals, semolina, and whole-meal flour.

Perhaps WGA's most disruptive effect is the way it hinders the body's ability to manage its supply of blood sugar. Insulin is a hormone that is vital for regulating many processes in the body. It is manufactured in the pancreas. Its production depends on the protein and sugars that you consume. It has one of the most vital functions to perform in the human body. We need an adequate quantity of it daily to function properly. Insulin moderates blood sugar levels. It does this by attaching itself to different types of cells. These cells include nerve cells, fat cells, and muscle cells. It orders them to let glucose inside themselves. Once the glucose is sufficiently consumed by the cells, the insulin lets go of it. When these cells receive glucose, they are able to function properly. They can efficiently carry out different processes like receiving messages from other chemical messengers as well as other different hormones and responding to them.

WGA comes along and disturbs the process. It has a notorious ability to mimic insulin in the body. It latches on to the fat cells specifically and sticks to them for an indefinite amount of time. Glucose then has a wide-open pathway to enter the cell, in far greater quantities than the cell is able to burn. This in turn results in increased production of fat as the body stores excess glucose as fat.

WGA can also attach to muscle cells. But here it resists any sort of sugar from going into the muscle cells. This causes muscle cells to be incapable of any healthy growth. They also cannot maintain themselves on account of receiving no fuel (i.e., the sugar cells). If this goes on, it can result in muscle wasting (Vasconcelos and Abreu Oliveira, 2004)[10].

WGA affects nerve cells in a similar process. It is theorized that WGA can park right on the insulin receptors that are present on the nerve cells. What ends up happening is that these cells continually send signals to your body that you are hungry. This happens because WGA is blocking the way by which they would get their fuel. They continually send signals to intake more food so that they can get the fuel and energy that they need to survive and function properly. Yet even if you consume a lot of calories, your nervous system will keep thinking that you are hungry since the nerve cells are facing a crisis of starvation brought on by WGA. Your fat cells will continue to increase even as nerve cells wither and die. The number of calories you take in will also escalate. Your brain cells will also lack energy which in turn causes brain fog. If left unchecked, slowly brain cells tend to die, leading to many other symptoms and diseases.

By comparison to the molecules of other lectins, WGA is not a large lectin. For this reason, it can enter the gut more easily than other lectins. Through the vagus nerve, WGA can soon get into your brain. Even blood-brain barriers are not a halt for WGA. As WGA is a sticky protein, things get even worse. It gets connected to other substances that the brain needs, leaving the brain without anything to do. Eventually, this imbalance will lead to neurological problems.

While causing harm to the brain, WGA will harm your body as well. This is when the issue of dual receptors becomes important. Your immune system is "tricked" to confuse foreign invaders with native tissues, and consequently autoimmune response happens.

WGA can harm blood vessels by connecting to the cells that line them. Once they do so, the immune system will mobilize to attack WGA, but ultimately blood vessels get attacked, and the result is hardened arteries. Hardened arteries lead to atherosclerosis.

Based on studies, WGA restrains cells from properly metabolizing vitamin D.

As you can see, WGA sets in motion a cascade of dysfunction and damage within the body.

Chapter 8: Lectin Sensitivity

Some commons symptoms are seen in people with lectin sensitivity. Basically, the level of lectin sensitivity will vary according to the individual's body condition. We'll mention the common symptoms below, and you can check whether you have any of them. The more the symptoms you have, the higher the sensitivity.

Adiponectin is identified as a marker for lectin and gluten sensitivity in humans by a study. The TNF-alpha level is recognized to act as a marker for exposure of lectin in individuals who are sensitive to those substances.

Here are the symptoms:

- Immune imbalances
- Abdominal discomfort
- Irritated GI tract
- Fatigue
- Excessive anxiety
- Brain fog
- OCD
- Skin problems such as eczema, fungus, psoriasis, and much moreetc.
- Hypoglycemic issues
- Joint and random pains
- Weight issues
- Migraines
- Water retention
- Sleep issues

So, these are the common issues in lectin-sensitive people. However, it is still not clear why some people are highly sensitive whereas some others aren't. There is continuous research regarding lectin sensitivity. But, the common reason is overactive nervous system.

Some people suffer from lectin allergy. The allergic reaction to lectins in this type of case is pretty obvious and severe. It also is an immediate reaction that confirms that lectins are the cause of their condition. There are also cases of people with abnormal sensitivity to lectins. Some people develop sensitivity due to genetic conditions as well. Those with compromised gastrointestinal systems can develop a sensitivity to lectins later in life.

The only way to get rid of your curiosity about lectin sensitivity is to go on a diet where you cut off all the lectin-containing foods from your diet. First, you have to get an accurate idea about food items that contain lectins. Lectins could be present in food in a variety of forms, so this part can be tricky. Lectins differ in type, impact, and potencies. So even if you suspect that lectins are to blame for unhealthy conditions in your body, there is plenty of work necessary to find out how they harm your body. After you have properly adopted a diet that is free from lectins, then work to reintroduce foods containing lectins into your diet slowly. You should do it one by one. If you really do have some sort of sensitivity to lectins, then the symptoms will become apparent.

Although there are many unknown factors, you can always work on your health. You can do your best to stay fit and healthy. By opting to follow a lectin-free diet or reducing lectin consumption, you may be able to improve your health. You may stop a self-destructive behavior and welcome a healthy life. Yet, going completely lectin-free is up to you. Make sure to do complete research when you opt for a new diet.

Chapter 9: Benefits Of A Lectin-Free Diet

Much of our conversation thus far has focused on the detrimental impacts of lectins. Yet in maintaining a balanced and objective perspective as we consider the benefits and drawbacks of a lectin-free diet, we cannot forget that some lectins are beneficial and necessary for healthy functioning of the body. And avoiding lectins would require us to completely remove several beneficial foods from our diets. In those cases, the losses probably outweigh the gains. So for most people, it's probably not wise to avoid lectins completely.

As we take note of both the positive and negative effects of lectins, it's important to understand the limitations of the scientific research that has been conducted. A higher percentage of research has been done on isolated lectins, but not on food lectins. That means that a quantity of concentrated lectins were given to subjects to see how they reacted. That leaves open the possibility that lectins, when consumed within the complex nutritional context of their source food, interact differently with the body than in the isolated situation in studies. Even that research has been carried out on animals or in test tubes and not on actual human beings, a further limitation to the scientific data available. So there is little to no credible research data for how food-based lectins affect human beings.

Still, there are strong arguments about the benefits of a lectin-free diet. When we refer to a lectin-free diet, we mean avoiding high-lectin foods like whole grains, quinoa, tomatoes, eggplant, legumes, and peppers. In their place, you will substitute or increase consumption of vegetables such as mushrooms, leafy greens, and broccoli and include other low-lectin foods in your diet.

These are the primary benefits of a lectin-free diet:

Reduction in the risk of peptic ulcers. Peptic ulcers are increased due to lectins. An ulcer is a wound created in the digestive tract. Usually, you'll find it in the stomach or a section of the esophagus. When you opt for a lectin-free diet, you reduce the risk of peptic ulcers.

Increase in energy. Once you move towards a lectin-free diet, you will feel a difference in your energy level. You will feel as if your mind and body are clear. Your energy level will be better than when you consume caffeine. You will be able to overcome issues such as tiredness, bloating, skin rashes, brain fog, and much more on the lectin-free diet.

Reduced inflammation and less pain. Joint pains will reduce over time because you are giving up foods with lectins.

Healing autoimmune diseases. High consumption of lectins has been connected to autoimmune diseases. Also, the gut's functioning is integral to the whole body, so when it is affected, dysfunction can blossom in a wide range of health problems. When the body's immune system does not have to fight invaders, it is able to rest, recuperate, and eliminate confusion that causes it to attack itself.

Help to reduce weight. It is theorized that lectins induce leptin resistance, leading to weight gain. The hormone leptin regulates the body's energy. Hence, when it is malfunctioning, you do not feel satiated. Your brain signals that you need to eat more, and you end up consuming more. Eventually, under such conditions, you will gain weight. Thus, another benefit of a lectin-free diet is that you can control your weight.

Recognition of lectin toxicity in foods. It is true that cooking can kill lectins, to some extent. For example, legumes are poisonous when eaten raw. Some people find them toxic because of their lectin level. This is the reason why it is better to avoid undercooked beans. When you become aware of the lectin-free diet, you understand the toxicity that lectins can cause in the body.

Benefits for people with food sensitivity. If you are someone who is highly sensitive to certain foods, you will likely benefit from a lectin-free diet. Usually, such people will face gastric distress once they consume a higher amount of lectins. Lectins are not digestible; they settle in the digestive tract and cause problems there. They also slow down metabolism. If you follow the lectin-free diet or reduce your intake of lectins, you will be able to protect your digestive tract from damage.

Research into lectins and the benefits of staying clear of them is ongoing. At this point, these benefits are considered the best.

The most important piece of information about the lectin-free diet is what you can eat. That's how you can get a proper picture of the diet. A sample of these foods is below. These are some of the foods that you must **consume in moderation or avoid** as much as possible.

Grains	Legumes	Nightshades	Dairy	Pseudo grains
Whole wheat bread Anything with gluten	Soybeans Peanuts Beans	Potatoes Peppers Paprika Tomatoes Eggplant	Yogurt Cheese Milk	Quinoa Brown Rice Certain seeds

If you are sensitive, you might react soon and face a lot of health problems so make sure to focus on what to eat and what not to! You must understand that you need lectins in your diet because they provide nutrients and some other health benefits. However, consuming too much can be dangerous.

Below are some of the common foods that are **permissible and beneficial** in a lectin-free diet.

Meats	Fruits	Vegetables	Nuts
Lobster Crab Turkey Beef Chicken	Apples Blueberries Dates	Broccoli Spinach Collard greens Swiss chard Kale	Almonds

As you can see, there are many common and enjoyable foods available when you are adhering to a lectin-free diet. Furthermore, these low or no-lectin foods provide a wide range of essential nutrients, ensuring that you will not starve or suffer from malnutrition on this eating plan. A lectin-free lifestyle can be accomplished in accordance with nutritional best practices, common sense, and without misery. In chapter 10, we will discuss in much greater detail what to eat and avoid while following a lectin-free diet.

Anyone could cite all of the studies and statistics in the world, but the crucial question for any life-changing decision is, Will it work for me? Is this thing worth trusting in? Ultimately, you will not have the answers to those questions until you run your own small-sample (of at least one!) experiment. You must give it a try to know what it actually contains and accomplishes. See whether you can prove that lectins are harming your mind and body. Most people do not make an effort to understand their health to this extent. Instead, they settle for health conditions that are less than ideal. They follow diets that make them miserable, that they can't stick to, and which don't produce lasting changes. Be different. Find out for yourself if you will benefit from a severe reduction in dietary lectins.

Chapter 10: Getting Started With A Lectin-Free Diet

Now that you have a basic understanding of lectins and their consequences for health, you can begin to focus on how to apply this information. Excessive consumption of lectins can cause digestive issues and chronic system inflammation in your body. So what can someone do to avoid these severe health dangers? The answer is pretty simple: avoid lectins. But it can be hard to eliminate lectins from your diet in "cold turkey" fashion, so what are the options you have?

How can you try the lectin-free diet in a meaningful way? First, commit yourself to the diet for a minimum time period that will enable you to assess whether there are benefits or drawbacks. Commit to following the diet without cheat days. Two weeks is probably a good starting point to get a proper understanding on how the diet affects your body. It can be tough at the beginning; but remember, you are utilizing the trial and error strategy. But, there are ways to fight against them, if you follow appropriate methods. Let's learn the techniques in detail and see the impact a lectin-free diet has.

You don't have to dedicate months. Just do it for weeks. If you do so, you should be able to figure out answers to your questions. You don't have to mess with all the variables. Be sure to find a decent plan that spells everything out for you and makes the diet as easy as possible. Once you have drawn your conclusions, if you find the diet helpful, then you can make long-term plans to remake your lifestyle, and your health, according to a lectin-free paradigm.

You must try it before recommending it to others so that you can confidently say that it works. If you follow the diet 100% without involving any cheat days, you could achieve an incredible result.

If you are sensitive to certain foods or if you don't know whether you are sensitive, it is better to try this diet for some time. The important thing that you must understand is to consume any foods and beverages at a moderate level. Even the healthiest food will become unhealthy if you consume it too much. It is always better to stay at a reasonable level.

A second way to get started that you can follow by itself or combine with the first idea is to simply reduce your consumption of lectins instead of completely eliminating them. Limiting such foods is not the only way to cut down on the amount of lectins that enter your system. There are several other ways to alter the foods you eat to drastically diminish their lectin content. Here are some suggestions you can consider:

Peeling and deseeding. Deseeding and peeling will reduce lectins to a great extent. Peeling fruits and vegetables reduces their lectin content from them. This is because most of the lectin is present in the skin of fruits and vegetables. You might have to be concerned when you are dealing with pumpkin, squash, tomatoes, and peppers.

Deseeding also results in the reduction of lectin content. This is important because there is a high concentration of lectins in seeds. Thus, it is better to avoid eating seeds as much as possible. Vegetables such as cucumbers, zucchini, pumpkins, and tomatoes will have much less lectin after they are deseeded.

Sprouting. When sprouting beans, grains, and seeds, the quantity of lectin content will reduce. The longer you sprout, the higher the rate of reduction in lectins. Lectins' deactivation depends on the plant's sprouting. The longer the time the plant is sprouted, the more deactivated its lectins will be. There is a massive decrease in lectin content as the beans, grains, and seeds are sprouted. This is because, in some beans and seeds, the lectin is present in the seed coat. As it matures, the seed coat metabolizes, and the lectin is effectively neutralized. So the threat that lies with the lectins is also neutralized.

It is not always the case that sprouting will cause a reduction in lectins, though. In some cases, sprouting increases the lectin content. For example, one plant that exhibits this opposite process is the alfalfa sprouts.

Soaking. If you think about how grandmas used to cook, you will see the difference clearly that much more effort was required for preparing ingredients before they were combined. They made sure to soak grains and beans before cooking. They soaked them really well and then rinsed them before they cooked the grains. Through this process, it is possible to reduce lectins. When you soak these food items in water, lectins leech out of the beans or grains and into the water in which they soak. Lectins are reduced by soaking the beans and grains. It is a tradition to first soak the seeds or beans for a long period before rinsing them and then finally cooking. Now you know what purpose this process serves.

To reduce lectins in beans and grains, soak them overnight, at least. You should also change the water often to prevent the lectins from saturating the water. Then before cooking, drain all of the water in which the food was soaked. Don't reuse that water for cooking as well. Also, rinse the legumes or beans effectively. Remember that any trace of the soaking water could contain lectins in high volumes, and it is a poisonous broth, so be sure to discard it.

According to some studies beans should be left to soak in water for approximately five hours. Then after being drained and rinsed, they should be boiled. The water used for boiling should be fresh, and beans should be boiled in it for thirty minutes at least. This two-part process of soaking and cooking utilizes two methods to remove or deactivate lectins.

Pro tip: add baking soda (sodium bicarbonate) to the water when you are soaking the grains so that it further reduces lectins. This addition will also help in destroying lectins even more.

Fermenting. Fermenting has a major benefit for us if we adopt this method to prepare our beans or legumes. It allows the good bacteria to dissolve and convert many of the harmful components of the food. This will convert harmful substances and helps digestion.

Human cultures that have grains in a lot of their dishes have developed various forms of fermentation. If we look at the healthiest populations, then we can find that many have fermented products as staples in their diets. Some popular fermented products are miso, tamari, tempeh, and natto. Sourdough bread and beer are also examples of fermented grains. Fermentation can also reduce the lectin quantity in dairy and vegetables.

Cooking. If you wish to reduce the lectin content in your diet, then cooking is the best way to reduce its effects. Most of the lectins in food can be deactivated by cooking thoroughly. For instance, cooking of the legumes in a high-pressure cooker eliminates nearly all the lectins present in them. In other food items that contain lectins, it can reduce the quantity. A tool like the Instant Pot can be useful, especially since boiling, baking, and drying are less effective when compared to pressure cooking.

Not all lectins are temperature sensitive. For example, grains are not.

Lectins bind with carbohydrates. When starches in lectins haven't been hydrolyzed by cooking, then the lectins will come in contact with the cells of the digestive tract. Otherwise, they bind with carbohydrates and don't irritate the digestive tract. They just pass through it instead. When the lectins interact with our digestive tract, it can cause the symptoms of food poisoning.

The nightshade vegetable family and many legumes that should not be eaten raw carry that precaution for for this exact reason. In the food's raw form, there are too many lectins and not enough carbohydrates to bind with them properly. The lectins in this case then gravitate toward the carbohydrates present in our cells, which is very harmful to us. When we cook the lectin-containing foods, we get a lot of floating carbohydrates which can bond with the lectins and effectively shuts off any harmful activity of free lectins. Cooking, first of all, destroys lectin, and if it doesn't do it fully, then excess carbohydrates basically render them useless.

It is impossible to eat beans or grain without cooking them first. Grains like quinoa (a protein rich seed) and rice are typically boiled before consumption.

Keep in mind that the same processes that deactivate and reduce lectins also do the same to beneficial vitamins and minerals in foods. Raw forms usually contain the highest quantities of nutrients.

Some seaweeds and mucilaginous vegetables bind lectins. This phenomenon makes the lectins nonexistent to the cells of the gut. In other words, no harm will be caused by lectins.

However, the unfortunate situation is that you will not be able to destroy lectins in certain grains even by using these methods. These methods are not effective for all types of lectins. There are stubborn lectins that will remain even if you use these treatments. Thus, you cannot entirely rely on these methods if you are naturally lectin intolerant. So if this is your situation, you will need a final strategy.

Be vigilant. This suggestion can vary from one person to another. What does being vigilant mean to you? I'd prefer not eating foods that are high in lectins. What if I am made to eat grains? Well, you can always pick white over whole grains. If you have to buy rice, consider buying white over brown rice. Try to avoid whole wheat as much as possible.

If you try a lectin-free lifestyle, see results, and like it, rather than manipulating and convincing your mind, you can give up those lectin-rich foods for good. And focus on living a healthy life!

Now that you are motivated to begin, let's look at some of the practical details you will need to succeed. As a starter, below are some of the common lectin-free food that you must incorporate to your life. Here we go:

Basil. You will find a wide variety of this plant, and it ranges from lemon, cinnamon, to cloves. This is categorized as a part of the mint plant. You will find ice creams and chocolates with a touch of basil. And don't forget that this is a natural repellent for insects.

Chocolate. The cacao bean is used to make chocolate by roasting. And chocolates are lectin-free so that you don't have to worry about eating them.

Dandelion Flowers. These are great for salad or to grind into smoothies. There are some other things such as zucchini, roses, violets, hibiscus, and much more. You can shop dandelions, but you must make sure that they are fresh.

Eggs. One egg includes vitamins B2, B6, B5, B12, A, E, K, D, zinc, selenium, phosphorus, folate, choline, and calcium. Of course, they have high cholesterol, but it does not increase bad cholesterol. You can try duck eggs as they make you fuller than any other eggs, so try them whenever possible.

Avocados. You can eat avocado every day because it is a botanical fruit. It has high fiber, so it is beneficial to your body. Avocados have high monounsaturated fat which helps to lower bad cholesterol. So, they are great for your heart, skin, brain, and many other organs.

Hemp. This is from the cannabis family, but this is not marijuana. There are many benefits from Hemp which also includes dietary and skin care products. This is one of the best vegan proteins for the ones who follow the lectin-free diet. This contains omega-3, vitamins B2, B1, A, E, and D, iron, and calcium. You can sprinkle this on soup or salad.

Olive Oil. If you can get farmer produced olive oil, you will be able to enjoy chemical free oil. This is considered the healthiest fat that helps to reduce inflammation. Olive oil enhances the linings of blood vessels, reduces blood pressure, avoids blood clots, and many other diseases related to the brain.

Quest Bars. If you are looking for a portable option, Quest Bars are ideal. I have mentioned a few options in the previous chapters, so you are offered with choices without having to sacrifice the taste.

Vinegar. It is essential to know that vinegar can be included in your lectin-free diet. As there are many options to choose from, you don't have to go for additional salad dressing. Different kinds of vinegar have various benefits, so it is recommended to include it to your diet.

Zinc. Foods such as sheep's milk, mushrooms, spinach, and cocoa powder are high in zinc. The minerals that act as antioxidants can be found with the help of zinc.

Here are some tips to consider to help you start well:

Begin by prepping your body to follow the diet. You are going to go start a diet
that your body is unfamiliar with. Of course, there will be changes. Your body will
experience differences, so you must prepare your body to accept it. So far, it has been
ingesting lectins, but now, you are going to stop lectin ingestion. Therefore, you must allow
your body time to adjust to the changes.

One of the must-know things is that if lectins' consumption is higher in your body, bad bacteria have probably taken control of the system. So, for some years, you have been satisfying your cravings in the wrong way. Thus, it can be tough to begin your lectin-free journey. This is one of the main reasons you could have setbacks.

Additionally, your gut might not be in good condition due to the influence of lectins. But, you don't
have to let it ruin your gut forever. It is time to take action; you must do what is required to make
your gut comply with the changes. When you change your diet, your gut will benefit.

However, it might take some time to witness changes. Once you start following the
diet, your gut bacteria will find balance, excess weight and inflammation will reduce, and you will experience additional benefits.

So, a damaged gut wall can take some time to repair itself. Thus, what can you do? Focus on cleansing it. When you cleanse it, your gut will get rid of harmful lectins. But, that's a good thing. To cleanse your system, you have to eat and avoid certain foods at a stretch for at least three days.

You must give up foods such as:

Sugar, soy, dairy, grains or pseudo-grains, seeds, Nightshade plants, wheat, roots, inflammatory oils, animal protein, and many others.

You must include foods such as:

Cruciferous, Brussels sprouts, broccoli, cauliflower, Bok choy, Swiss chard, Kale Collards, Kimchi, arugula, cabbage, onions, celery, carrots, scallions, leeks, chives, chicory, beets, artichokes, radishes, cilantro, leafy greens, garlic, and many other lectin-free veggies.

However, the foods that I have mentioned are powerhouses. These will do their duty to pump out lectins that were invading your body. The veggies are great, so you can eat as much as you prefer. But for the ones with IBS and gut issues, it is better to make sure that veggies are thoroughly cooked. Even though vegetables are great, you must ensure that they are organic.

You must not forget to include proteins, healthy oils, and fats. When considering oils, avocado oil can be added every day, but there are options such as olive oil, flaxseed oil, coconut oil, and hemp oil.

Everything is alright, but what if you want to enjoy a snack? You might crave snacks while you are cleansing your body. You can consider eating half an avocado while adding a pinch of olive oil and lemon juice. And also, you can add approved nuts to spice it up. However, there are many blogs online where you can find snacks for lectin-free dieters so make sure to read them!

So, that's all about cleansing your body. But, you must not forget to get good sleep as it is one of the essential things for a healthy lifestyle. I don't want to give hope saying that cleansing is natural. But, it will get easier over time. You have to give your best, yet don't try to achieve everything at once. If you do the needful to your body, it will recover soon to follow the lectin-free diet. But then, don't revert to your bad habits right after cleansing your body. If you do so, there will not be a positive result. Once you have purged lectins out of your body, get started with the diet! Don't step back!

If you don't try, you will never achieve. Also, if you want to be healthy, you must take the necessary steps towards it. Don't ever undermine the importance of following a proper diet. Certain diseases will not show up sooner, but over time, you might find many illnesses that you never thought you had. These sudden revelations often happen when you don't care about the food that you eat. Your body is fragile; hence, you must take good care of it. Of course, it might be hard to be 100% healthy or to avoid all the unhealthy foods. But, you must, at least, try to limit the unhealthy consumption.

Who wants to live an unhealthy life? How can you live peacefully when you have gut problems, inflammation, and IBS? They can get worse over time. Hence, you must make sure to treat such diseases as soon as possible. The saying goes "prevention is better than cure." Isn't it? So, focus on preventing instead of worrying about the cure once you are unwell.

Chapter 11: What To Eat And Avoid While Following A Lectin-Free Diet

If you have given a lectin-free diet a trial run and are ready to commit for a longer term, you will need a great deal more information to guide your grocery shopping trips and kitchen stocking.

So, now, let's get started with the foods that you must eat and avoid when you go lectin-free.

Foods that you must eat	Foods that you must avoid
Olive oil	Potato chips
Algae oil	Potato
Coconut oil	Bread
MCT oil	Pasta
Macadamia oil	Rice
Grass-fed ghee	Pastries
Avocado oil	Cookies
Rice bran oil	Tortillas
Perilla oil	Pastries
Sesame oil	Cereal
Walnut oil	Dairy
Red palm oil	Yogurt (Greek yogurt too)
Avocados	Cottage cheese

Kiwis	Sugar
Berries	Diet drinks
Baobab fruit	Peas
Green Plantains	Legumes
Rutabaga	Chickpeas (Hummus too)
Parsnips	Green beans
Cassava	Tofu
Yucca	Soy
Taro roots	Soy protein
Persimmon	Edamame
Tiger nuts	Pea protein
Green Papaya	Textured vegetable protein
Green Mango	Beans and lentils
Millet Sorghum	Cucumbers
Broccoli	Squashes
Cruciferous	Eggplant
Cauliflower	Melons
Napa Cabbage	Tomatoes
Brussels Sprouts	Chili peppers
Bok Choy	Bell peppers
Swiss Chard	Chia
Collards	Cashews
Chinese Cabbage	Peanuts
Arugula	Grains

Kale	Wheat
Celery	Quinoa
Leeks	Oats
Onions	Brown rice
Chicory	Barley
Carrots	Corn and corn products
Scallions	Popcorn
Artichokes	Barley and wheat grass
Radishes	Soy oil
Beets	Grape seed
Okra	Cottonseed
Garlic	
Asparagus	
green leaf lettuce	
Spinach	
Romaine	
Butter lettuce	
Escarole	
Endive	
Parsley	
Fennel	
Mizuna	
Basil	
Algae	

Mint
Sea vegetables
Seaweed
Mushrooms
Pecans
Walnuts, pine nuts, and pistachios (in moderation)
Hemp seeds
Coconut
Sesame Seed
Brazil nuts
Fish
Canned tuna
Salmon
Shrimp
Lobster
Crab
Oyster
Sardines
Anchovies
Olives
Crustacean shells
Dark chocolate
Goat butter and cheese

Ghee	
Sheep brie	
Coconut yogurt	
Organic sour and heavy cream	
Whey protein (lectin-free)	
Pasture-raised poultry	
Chicken	
Ostrich	
Turkey	
Omega 3 eggs	
Goose	
Duck	
Meat	
B-up Bars	
Quest Bars	
Pottentia bars	
MariGold bars	
Larabars	

The table includes what to eat and avoid when following the lectin-free diet. But I have not included ALL the foods, just the common ones. When you go through this table, you will get some understanding. And you can research more to find the foods that you can and cannot eat as a lectin-free dieter. Remember to consume any food in moderation.

If you can remember the foods that are high in lectin, you should find it easier to avoid them. So, what are they? Generally, legumes and grains have a higher rate of lectins. Certain foods can be consumed after pressure cooking. Nightshades, squashes, nuts and seeds, and some vegetables also contain a higher rate of lectins. So it is your responsibility to avoid them as much as possible.

Sometimes, it is tough to remain disciplined when you follow a diet. But being hard on yourself will not provide positive results. You will not be able to avoid foods that are rich in lectins in a day or two. Sometimes, they might be your favorite foods. Hence, it might be difficult for you to give up those. So, what should you do? Check out the following tips. These tips might help you stay on track when following the lectin-free diet.

Begin with attainable expectations. You might love the lectin-free diet, but that doesn't mean you can set unattainable goals. For example, you plan to ditch all the foods that are rich in lectin and to move to a lectin-free diet today. Try to be practical and think whether you can do that in reality. Even if you give up lectin-rich foods, it might not last long. Hence, you must focus on the things that are attainable. Setting achievable goals helps to follow the diet without setbacks.

Keep lectin-rich foods out of sight. It can be tough to avoid lectin-rich foods. Even if you are ready to leave them, some of your family members might not be ready to avoid those. And you can't force your family members, but you can explain it to them. Still, if they are not prepared to give up those foods, you must keep them out of sight. When something is out of your sight, it will not be in your mind. When you see something, you might feel like eating it, so you will not be able to follow this diet or stay healthy. If you follow this tip, you will be able to continue your journey.

Focus on the motivations. When you know the reason why you must follow the lectin-free diet, it will be easy to move towards it. But, if someone forces you, then you might not feel like following it or will not understand the value. Similarly, you must remember the reason why you selected to go lectin-free, and it will help you to move forward. Try to jot down the reasons why you have chosen this diet and focus on the benefits that you will get. When you do this, you can have a look at those whenever you feel like giving up. Motivation is crucial to following a diet successfully.

Don't be hard on yourself. Assume that you have no other choices than eating those foods that you wanted to avoid. What are you going to do? Are you going to avoid those and remain hungry? Even if you do, you will be frustrated and angry. A diet is essential to maintain good health, but mental well-being is even more critical. Also, remember, it is okay to have cheat days. Yes, we mentioned not to have cheat days, but that's when you follow the diet in a trial run. For the long term, cheat days will provide you with pleasant incentives, so long as you are determined not to get off track, or if you will balance them off properly. If you are hard on yourself, you might give up following the lectin-free diet totally because it will be frustrating. Hence, try to be vigilant when you are in such a situation.

Don't give up on healthy eating. Sometimes things go crazy when you are traveling. When you are home, you don't have to worry about giving up lectin-rich foods. But, when you are traveling, you might have to deal with specific issues. You might even grab something when you are too hungry to worry about lectins. Usually, you'd be left with the option of processed food, and it is unhealthy. If you are going to travel for some time, make sure to plan your meals accordingly. Do a quick search before your journey about finding lectin-free food while traveling. If you do so, you don't have to give up on healthy eating. Also, it will help you to follow the diet without a break.

Track your progress. It is always better to keep an eye on how you are improving. Even when you are achieving your life goals, you must keep track of the progress. Similarly, when you are following the lectin-free diet, make sure to track your progress. When you know how you progress, it will help you keep moving. For example, if you see changes in stomach bloating, and if you don't have it as you had before, jot it down. When you look at it, you might feel like continuing the diet. It is a great mechanism to keep going.

Ask someone to join. When you follow a diet alone, it can be pretty tough. You might not have the energy or the interest to follow the diet in the long term. But, when you have someone else who is following the lectin-free diet, it will be like teamwork. There will be encouragement, support, and a team effort. Hence, try explaining the diet to your friend or spouse. And make them join you so that you can carry out the diet easily and bring positive changes to your life.

These tips will provide support to kick-start your diet if it suits you. Even if it doesn't, you might have to reduce lectin consumption. So for that, you can utilize some of these tips. Whenever you are following a new diet, it is essential to find ways to keep moving. Nobody likes to have restrictions on food. But, if you want to live a healthy life, it is essential to consider healthy foods. The best way to consume healthy food is to follow a proper diet. Once you follow a diet for some time, it will eventually become a habit. And you will not go off track in the long run. However, it is all about practice, perseverance, and consistency.

Here are some additional tips and bits of information to help you succeed on a lectin-free diet:

- Lectins are dry heat resistant substances. Raw legume flour is sometimes used in baked goods. It should be used with caution because it has the potential to irritate your gut and cause other problems related to lectins.
- As a means of escaping the harmful effects of lectins, some might prefer a paleo diet which focuses on vegetables and fruits rather than beans and grains. The lectin-free diet helps

you avoid lectins in your diet, resulting in a healthy life, yet it does so without as much restriction as a paleo diet.

- There are 2.1 billion people who are overweight or obese. This figure makes up about one-third of the world's population (Zauderer, 2019)[11]. What is the main cause that makes people of the world this unhealthy? Many experts and people with experience in health-related issues say it is inflammation.

Our diets today contain some common causes of inflammation:

- Sugar
- White flour
- Preservatives
- Chemical additives
- Corn syrup rich in fructose
- Trans fats

The question of whether lectins are harmful has been repeatedly asked in this eBook. The simple answer is that it varies. It varies based on the lectin type, concentration, and the individual. People who face issues such as autoimmune disease, inflammation, and many other health problems must avoid lectins as much as possible. Certain seeds are unhealthy for some people, but it is a rarity. However, most studies on people with autoimmune disease and inflammation display positive results when they follow the lectin-free diet.

Chapter 12: Success With The Lectin-Free Diet

The lectin-free diet has caused controversy with some nutritionists for quite a while now. However, the disagreements between different nutritionists found a turning point when numerous success stories started coming in with regards to the lectin-free diet. People who have been following lectin-free diet plans shared their success stories on social forums and highlighted the positive aspects of eliminating lectins from their diet plans. These successful stories helped in getting a clearer picture of lectin-free diets as the continuous controversy affected its positive standpoint among the general public.

Perhaps no individual has inspired a more profound change in opinion about the lectin-free diet than Kelly Clarkson, the famous singer. She was a patient of Dr. Steven Gundry and followed the principles of the Plant Paradox Diet. Her transformation was the most talked about topic around town since after adopting the Plant Paradox Diet she was able to lose approximately 37 pounds of weight within a one-year period. Before this, she was struggling with weight issues and nothing actually helped her in getting the desired result. However, after changing her eating habits as per the Plant Paradox Diet, she was able to get rid of all the unwanted fat. It also helped her in dealing with inflammation issues[12].

So the question is what made Kelly Clarkson choose this specific diet among others? Kelly was diagnosed with thyroid and autoimmune disease, and she needed a well-planned diet. Her plan never included to "lose weight" as a criterion for success; she was rather interested in dealing with her medical conditions through natural ways instead of going on medications. The best point that she indicated in one of her interviews was that she never used medicine for her medical conditions after February 2018, which in itself is a huge win for her. Another point which made Kelly use this diet was the claim made by Dr. Gundry that many lectins and protein-containing foods are mainly responsible for most of the health-related ailments, from unnecessary weight gain and fats to thyroid issues. The Plant Paradox Diet is credited for helping Kelly in reversing the complications caused by lectins.

Another helpful strategy that Dr. Gundry employs in his book The Plant Paradox is featuring a patient success story in each chapter. These provide real-life examples of people who suffered with chronic conditions, applied the principles of the Plant Paradox Diet, and experienced life-changing improvements. In no way are these guarantees that any other person will achieve the same results. But when taken at face value (instead of read cynically as fictional mock-ups), these stories present a fraction of the many successes Dr. Gundry has observed in the avoidance of lectins.

To break the ice on a tenuous point, it is important to highlight that most of the food items traditionally considered as healthy contain lectins, including vegetables, grain, and fruits. This may sound absurd, but the research done by Dr. Gundry has highlighted a different side of healthy foods which subsequently has raised concerns for some of the nutrition experts.

Most of the food items consumed by Americans are processed, which affects their health. Kelly indicated that she adhered to the Plant Paradox Diet by eliminating all the processed food from her daily regimen, which helped help her in reducing inflammation issues and fighting back against thyroid concerns, as well. This step alone is considered almost universally as a necessary step in any serious diet plan. Even if we set aside a lectin-free diet or the Plant Paradox Diet, people can significantly boost their health just by eliminating all types of processed and junk food from their meals. Kelly's case is just one among many other success stories. For people who are double-minded about adopting the Plant Paradox Diet, you can start off by reducing the amounts of foods that contain lectins or by cooking them thoroughly to lessen their harmful impacts on the health. This will help their metabolism in adjusting with new patterns and would further allow them to eradicate those food items entirely from their routine that contains a high amount of lectins.

The Expensive Side Of The Plant Paradox Diet

The Plant Paradox Diet may seem like a normal weight-loss diet to many, yet it's quite the opposite. The diet may cost you a fortune, if not planned properly. This may come as a surprise for many, but eating healthy food on a strict diet costs you more than regularly spending on fast foods and processed convenience foods. Before starting off with the Plant Paradox Diet, it is important to understand the costs and how they affect your budget. Even Kelly Clarkson mentioned in one of her interviews that the Plant Paradox Diet is really expensive to do, and she couldn't have afforded it before as she comes from a poor family. Initially, the costs of the diet will affect your overall budget, and it could get difficult to hold onto your essential grocery items. However, with extra planning and proper strategy you can actually start the Plant Paradox Diet without hurting your budget. This may take some time initially, but once you are prepared with the planning, it will cost you less and help you in making a healthy change. And the extra costs of food now are nothing to be compared with the astronomical costs of health care to treat chronic problem later in life.

To begin with, it is vital to divide the grocery list into three sections: seasonal list, monthly list, and a weekly list. This would work as a great starting point for those who want to keep up with the diet plan without affecting their budget. For the seasonal list, before the start of each season, make sure to create a list of all the mandatory items that you will need, and purchase them in huge quantities, including fish, poultry, and wholesale food items—you can always freeze them for months. Moving ahead with the monthly list, at the beginning of each month, make a list of all those common items that you use in daily cooking, including olive oil, spices, and herbs, sauces and pesto, butter and nuts. These items can be used for months, as they are used in small portions for cooking. Lastly, the weekly list. If you have successfully conquered the first two major lists, then managing a weekly list won't be an issue. Just make a weekly list at the start of each week by adding the necessary items such as eggs or dairy products which you will need on a weekly basis. Other than these, you will already have the seasonal items in your freezer and common food items in your kitchen as they were already planned. Strategic planning would definitely allow you to stay consistent with your lectin-free diet without affecting your budget. This would also enable you to keep track of your food portions and expenses overall. Another way to save your money and avoid being on the expensive side is to buy from discount stores and farmers' markets. These two places are heaven for all those who wish to start a diet plan without spending hundreds of dollars each week. Discount stores are worth a visit as they contain almost everything you may need for your diet plan, including organic food options.

Some of the other cost-savings tips for the Plant Paradox Diet plan are as follows:

Meat vs. No Meat – If you are vegetarian, you are good to go. Even if you are a non-vegetarian, you should commit to just one meat-meal per day. Start with this pattern and once you get hold of it try to go one to two days without meat. There is always a substitute. Make yourself adaptable to these new eating patterns.

Stick to the List – Make sure to not buy anything that's not necessary or not mentioned on your list. Just stick to your lists that you have made for the week or month.

Mix in Meat – If you are persistent in using meat in your meals and can't go a day without adding meat to at least one meal, then try to stretch the meat by mixing it with vegetables. For example, you can make chicken and cauliflower cutlets by mixing them together. This will allow you to stretch your meat for a longer period of time and you won't have to buy meat very often.

Chapter 13: An Evaluation Of The Lectin-Free Diet

Does it do more harm than good?

According to some doctors and experts, the lectin-free diet may be causing more harm than good. Cutting out such a large variety of food is bound to leave us deficient in many nutrients that are readily present in those items. There is not a lot of research that proves or backs the theory that lectins are as bad as claimed. So we cannot go on living lectin-free just based on little hypothesis and information. The lectin free diet is not adequately supported by facts but mainly based on theory instead.

Many nutritional experts point out the fact that till now there isn't any science-based literature that classifies lectin as the main culprit of numerous human ailments. Some say that the main goal behind this movement is profit. The individuals benefiting from this movement are selling the theory and making money off of the supplements and diet plans. There is not enough evidence to back up the claims of all the positive effects of the lectin-free diet. The author of The Plant Paradox also sells lectin shield capsules. They are sixty-six cents per capsule. The lectin shield is said to aid you in resisting the lectin influx in your body. It essentially protects the body against lectins and any kind of effects it has.

There are always trends of diets that come one after another. Gluten-free, paleo, and keto are a few examples of trendy diets that have recently enjoyed popularity. Going to the grocery store would result in a headache if one would follow these diets in turn. They may be red herrings that diminish eventually.

Unfortunately, many people fall for them. Before lectin came under fire, wheat and fat which identified as causes of so many health troubles that we face. If eliminating these things from diets helped people, they are exceptions. Everyone's body works in different ways. If eliminating a thing from a meal made someone feel better, then it doesn't become a universal truth that it will work for anybody else who is facing a similar issue. If you plan to follow a diet to cure a certain health problem, then you must know there is a big possibility it won't work for you.

Lectins are mainly found in food items that have always been considered beneficial to human health. So there is justified disbelief amongst people about claims that lectins are harmful.

The author of the book that promotes the lectin-free diet, Dr. Gundry, claims to have lost 70 pounds by following the lectin-free diet regime. He says that the only thing people need to take care of is removing all the major lectin sources. They will start to lose weight despite not cutting down their calories. They still eat the same amount of calories but only reduce lectin-containing substances from their diet. Dr. Gundry explains that despite consuming lots of calories, they are not storing it as fat anymore.

One of the main objectives of following a lectin-free diet plan is for weight loss. Yet, there are many studies that have actually proven that lectins aid in weight loss. Whole grains, especially, have been linked with weight loss. A study also tested subjects who were given a diet of pulses for a total of six weeks. Those subjects have lost a great deal of weight as compared to other subjects who didn't consume any pulses (Kim et al., 2015)[13].

One major caution about the lectin-free diet is that people already consume so few healthy fruits and vegetables. If anything, they should eat more of these type of items. Only 10 percent of Americans eat the recommended fruit and vegetable quantity daily. That is a worryingly low figure. It also tells us how little we may need to worry about lectin and its disadvantages. In contrast to vaguely theorized harmful effects of lectins, there are proven benefits of many lectin-containing fruits and vegetables. Perhaps the majority of people should eat the diet that has been traditionally understood as healthy before we rush to the conclusion that it doesn't work.

Any type of diet that puts a compulsory ban on commonly eaten food can put a person under the risk of anxiety and stress. These symptoms can be brought on by wracking our brains to produce suitable, healthy meals based on individual budgets. One who is following a diet might also be extremely sensitive about his health issues, and he could be unnecessarily strict on himself.

It can cause a sort of food fear. This may derail us from our healthy ways toward a disaster. It is easy to get caught up in food choices, especially when we become overly concerned about them. We may end up putting too much blind faith in nutrition science which could be troublesome for us.

It is true that nutrition science is mostly driven by money. Often studies are sponsored by investors who back an outcome that they are interested in. The true discoveries and objective studies are left to collect dust because no one is interested in them. Instead of searching about the truths, researchers today are focused on making their study follow the latest trends that are currently being followed. The lure of fame and wealth drive what is reported. As of now, lectins are under scrutiny. So all the results of the studies will be aimed toward proving its harmful and negative effects.

Some people worry themselves so much about the apparent "toxins" present in common meals that it could potentially lead them to develop some kind of disorder. In many cases, eating disorder starts from exactly this kind of behavior. Eating food becomes sort of a chore to find the healthiest and "free of any toxins" items. In people's searches, they become highly critical of any sort of food presented to them. Every single food item has its benefits as well as its harmful effects. The harmful effects mostly appear under very specific conditions. Customarily, we cannot control all the environmental conditions in which we live. We can try our best, but being paranoid will only make life difficult for us. So it is better to relax and not worry about vague information—unless and until it is proven to have a certain effect which will cause you harm.

The media's new trend for dieting is the lectin-free diet, thanks in part to Kelly Clarkson. Yet, many lectin-containing foods, such as legumes and whole grains pack a lot of nutrients. They are good sources of iron, fiber, and vitamin B. These nutrients are hard to find in some restrictive diets. Most, if not all, lectin-concentrated foods are thoroughly cooked one way or another. Cooking those leaves only a trace amount of lectin, which is almost negligible. For a vast amount of people, cooked lectins in food are safe for consumption. The negative effects of some trace amounts of lectin are heavily outweighed by the positive nutritional value of those food items.

The Facts And True Theory About Lectins

Because of new trends, lectins are being irrationally blamed for causing severe chronic illnesses. This is an attractive solution if you have diagnosed yourself with an illness that is mysterious in its origin and its effects. After hearing about lectins and "the plant paradox," you may find appeal in the possibility that lectins are the real root cause behind your mystery ailment.

Unfortunately, the theory of chronic illnesses is not well explained and confusing. People who suffer from chronic illnesses don't get any closer to the cure because of random facts about nutrition. The link between chronic illness and certain diets and specific foods is so misleading. Blindly believing whatever latest nutrition discovery you come across will end up with you raising your hopes for something that is not entirely true. If you chose to follow the modern trends in hopes of bettering your condition, then you will meet with not only disappointment but perhaps also harm. It is because you would have neglected the foods that may actually be providing you the essential nutrients.

So many people today are of the opinion that carbohydrates are bad. They don't consider anything beyond that. There are actually healthy carbohydrates present as well. The bias against carbohydrates is part of the reason they believe the lectin theory.

Fruit fear is spread because lectins are found in these foods, as well. If we take a look back at history, many people have claimed that they were healed from unknown illnesses by consuming fruits and vegetables. Yet now the newest claim is that fruits and vegetables are the cause of chronic illnesses thanks to the lectin theory. Many people suffering from RA and MS make potatoes the main element of food in their diet. There are multiple cases of people recovering from those conditions with diets full of lectin-containing items.

We must be aware that pathogens are the real villains that cause illnesses.

Chapter 14: Benefits Of Lectins

There is a host of positive impacts from the consumption of lectins and the foods that contain them, particularly when consumption is not excessive.

- They help in regulating cell adhesion in our body.
- Some studies show that lectins contain anticancer properties.[14]
- Lectins also aid in synthesizing glycoproteins for the body.
- Lectins can also protect us against infection. Lectins contain antimicrobial properties, and they keep us safe from diseases caused by infection. HIV-1 in test tubes was repressed by a lectin which was obtained from a banana.
- Beans contain a lot of lectins. People who incorporate them into their daily diets effectively have a sufficient amount of fiber and minerals available to them. They also are less likely to gain an extra amount of weight. Consumption of beans also helps to regulate blood pressure.
- Tomatoes are a good source of a robust antibiotic, carotenoid lycopene. It helps safeguard our skin against the UV rays which can cause major skin damage. Tomatoes also have a number of benefits for our cardiovascular health. A lowered risk of stroke is found to be linked to high levels of lycopene in the blood. Premature death is however linked to having a low level of blood lycopene.
- Lectins help regulate the immune system of the body. It helps us to fight against harmful pathogens. If we are sick with pneumonia, lectins help us battle against it. Lectins are said to be immune-stimulants. Bitter melon herbs contain lectins that provide this benefit.

- Herbs contain lectins that are extremely beneficial. The herbs that belong to the bean family have a very high level of lectins. These include astragalus, carob, and kudzu.
- They are effective in the reduction of the glycemic effect of the food we eat. It slows down the process of carbohydrate digestion or stops it. That could be a contributor to weight loss. It could also be a factor in lessening the risk of diabetes.
- Beans are identified as the food that has shown to have the foremost connection in lowering the rates of breast cancer according to a study ("The Real Story on Lectins," 2019)[15].
- Beans have a very large amount of antiphytochemicals. The way lectins bind to carbohydrates and slow down their digestion could actually be linked to their anti-cancer properties. Plants also contain phytate which is also thought to fight cancer.
- Like beans, mushrooms are also determined as one of the foods that resist cancer. There is also research in progress about the potential of lectin-based foods use for certain cancer therapies.
- Plant food lectins may also help in blocking the activity of certain angiogenesis promoting lectins on the cells of the human body. This phenomenon also results in preventing cancer.
- Some weight loss is observed in animals due to common legume lectins. Cholecystokinin (CCK) is recognized as the hormone whose secretion is possibly the cause of weight loss. The activation of orexin can also affect appetite and wakefulness. CCK causes digestive enzymes and bile to be released. CCK can mitigate hunger and also the rate the stomach gets rid of food. CCK also decreases the secretion of stomach acid which then slows the process of digestion.

Ayurveda and Traditional Chinese Medicine

History and widespread use across cultures are also on the side of lectins. The ayurvedic diet makes good use of legumes and grains. Lectin-rich foods have been used for thousands of years in traditional Chinese medicine. Legumes are actually considered to be astringent to the palate. It means that they produce a drying sensation. They satisfy the stomach and repress appetite. Legumes are advised to be soaked prior to consumption. By doing this, their antinutrient content is reduced, but it elevates their nutritional value.

In traditional Chinese medicine, beans are believed to aid in reducing swelling and can also carry out the removal of toxins. They are thought to have a neutral effect on the balance of the body.

Tomatoes are considered to have a cooling effect. It promotes detoxification in the body and aids in digestion.

Chapter 15: Risks Of A Lectin-Free Diet

A Lectin-Free Diet?

Many nutritionists agree that the benefits of lectins heavily outweigh whatever the harms it poses. By taking both the pros and cons into consideration, one can come to a rational conclusion. Let's take the fruits and vegetables that are banned in the lectin-free diet. They provide essential vitamins and minerals that are proven to be a basic requirement of the human body. If the risk of having a troubled gastrointestinal tract from consumption of a small amount of lectins is proven, then those food items are still worth the troubles. They are essential to humans. The risk is not proven and is still only in theory, so it is naive to cut out essential nutrient-packed foods from our diets. If we are having little troubles here and there regarding inflammation and stomach ailments, then removing some important foods from our meals carelessly could spell more troubles for us in the long run.

The harmful effects it does pose are under very specific circumstances. They are not to be ignored though and should be taken notice of. All experts and nutritionists are not on board with the lectin free diet and wonders it entails. A lot of research has to go into deciding whether it is truly harmful and the cause of many ailments. People tend to adopt a certain diet because it serves a purpose. The main purpose of a lectin-free diet, at least according to Gundry, is that it reduces the weight of the body and reduces inflammation.

The lectin-free diet tends to remove all the lectin-containing food items from regular meals. Common comestibles that contain lectins are; conventionally grown poultry and meat, nightshade vegetables, dairy, grains, legumes, and quinoa.

Some studies do show some evidence of the benefits that are achieved by going lectin-free. Main advantages are for cardiovascular disease and metabolic syndrome. The conditions that are helped by reducing lectins in the diet are as follows:

- High blood sugar levels
- High blood pressure
- Surplus weight around the waist
- High cholesterol levels

After some testing, it was found out that some patients with IBS (irritable bowel syndrome) showed progress in weight loss when lectin-containing foods were eliminated from their diets. They followed a low FODMAP diet. In this diet, lectin-containing substances such as starchy vegetable and beans are not to be consumed.

Plant-Based Diet And Lectin Quantity

A plant-based diet generally consists of lectin-containing foods. They are healthy foods as we have always known them to be. The seven main ingredients of a plant-based diet are:

1. Zucchini.

2. Quinoa. It has a very high amount of lectin content.

3. Nuts. Especially peanuts and cashews. They have a large and potent type of lectins present in them.

4. Rice (brown).

5. Beans. The peas and lentils have a high amount of lectins present in them.

6. Potatoes.

7. Tomatoes. The nightshade family of vegetables has been identified as having a substantial amount of lectins present in them. Squashes also belong in the group that has a high amount of lectin as well as sugar. They should be taken with care.

Vegetable oil such as sunflower oil, corn, and soybean oil are also food items that contain lectins. Casein A1 protein is found in organic and grass-fed dairy products. It is not considered to be very healthy.

What the lectin-free diet proposes is to get rid of them. There are new arguments that have surfaced in Gundry's book that labels them as containers of hidden toxins. They are linked to causing much inflammation-related problems in people. These problems also lead to bigger health concern such as diabetes and cancer.

Disadvantages Of A Lectin-Free Diet

A lectin-free diet doesn't essentially hurt you, but it doesn't do you any favors either. There seems to be little truth in articles and knowledge that is floating around about it. People are not searching more about it and instead choosing to believe in stories right before their eyes.

All those food items that this diet bans have a long history of being nutritious and important for human health. They are some of the best sources of fiber that are readily available to us. Fiber is proven to be important for maintaining good health. It plays an important role in lowering the risk of heart disease and maintaining an ideal weight. Fiber also helps in stabilizing blood sugar levels.

In one particular circumstance, the lectin-free diet is advisable. Although it is not proven, you should give the lectin-free diet a chance if no other diet plan has yet worked for you. If you are facing digestive troubles, and you have already tried other diets like gluten and FODMAPs, and they haven't helped you in any way, then there is no reason to not give the lectin-free diet a chance as well. It is still recommended that you get help from an expert dietician. They will make sure you get proper nutrients even by eliminating essential food groups from your diet.

Think about it yourself. On the one hand, you have a low-fat, healthy diet that is based mostly on natural ingredients and plants versus a diet that is mostly based on supplements and meat. The latter is the lectin-free diet, and the former is the normal healthy balanced diet. The lectin-free diet also pushes you toward more fatty food items, which doesn't sound like a good idea. You should not experiment with your health like that without proper guidance.

As of yet, there is not sufficient evidence that can classify the lectin-free diet as a healthy one. A healthy diet is based on sustainability and whether it provides you a full spectrum of nutrients that you require in order to stay healthy. The nutrients include all the major vitamins and minerals. It also means that on that diet, a person can thrive and live for the rest of their lives. A lectin-free diet eliminates such a large number of nutritious foods and makes one dependent on supplements to fulfill their basic needs. It doesn't make this diet a sustainable option for a longer period of life.

A good and healthy life calls for balance in our diets. We should not rely on one type of thing just because of its benefits that we learned from the internet. We should incorporate all food types in our diets as much as we can.

Lectin As Antinutrient

Lectins are a group of proteins that is commonly referred to as antinutrients. Lectins help plants from being digested. They protect the plants from predators. The antinutrients group also includes fibers. The anti-nutrients role in human health is actually unclear as they aren't nutrients. The main purpose lectins serve in animals is that it helps in cell binding. They are responsible for recognizing the carbohydrates present on the surface of other cells. They bind with each other through this process. In plants, the purpose is widely believed to be its defensive mechanism. It protects the plant against many insects and pathogens as well.

Antinutrients, as the name suggests, resist or disturb the process of nutrient absorption in the body. Many experts believe that many antinutrients are actually good for humans despite their widely known name and function. So quickly putting down any lectin is not advisable just yet. There isn't any foolproof evidence that should cement that as a hard-known truth.

Chapter 16: Myths About Lectins

From the time humans first appeared on earth and till now, our diets have changed a great deal. Just like animals, our food has domesticated. Our food items have also undergone the process of natural selection.

Our current diets already have minimized the number of vegetables and lectin-based foods. We don't seem any healthier than our ancestors, but the opposite can be stated as truth. Our ancestors were much healthier than us. Our diet is becoming unhealthy with the abundance of meat and processed wheat. People today have fewer plants in their diet as it is.

Some of the nightshades like potatoes and tomatoes were once poisonous. They were then farmed to be suitable for human consumption. They became bigger in size and much sweeter. Of course, they also become less poisonous. Tomatoes and potatoes contained chemical substances solanine and tomatine respectively. They were the lethal chemicals that were extremely toxic to humans.

The sweetest food you could find was only as sweet as a carrot is. Tomatoes used to be as small as berries. So many advancements have been made in terms of food that at one point in history kale, broccoli, brussels sprouts, cauliflower, and cabbage all used to be one single vegetable.

You can say that foods are undergoing evolution. However, the ones that were once toxic and harmful must carry some trace amounts of those substances till this day. We have also been adapting ourselves to these food items along the way. In some cases, we have developed immunity to the toxins in some foods and learned to thrive on its benefits.

The Controversial Diet

Some people who have supported the lectin-free diet may have eradicated some other food items other than lectins. That may have positively affected them, and the lectin-free diet was given all the credit. The real reason for their better health may be something else entirely. The lectin-free diet also calls for the removal of heavily processed foods from our diet. Elimination of them from one's diet alone results in a number of positive health benefits.

People who consume junk foods regularly in their diet don't have the best of health. They may be in their middle ages, and they will be encountering health problems that are supposed to be brought on by old age. When they stop consuming all the junk and processed foods, they readily feel better, as well they. One of the biggest positive impacts it has on health is weight loss.

Many of the world's traditional populations have thrived on a diet that is mostly lectin-based. This makes the lectin-free diet very controversial.

Diets that are not sustainable are not worthwhile. When one is on a certain diet and they feel very restricted with it, then as soon as the time of diet expires, they go back to their old eating habits. That is where their problems start reappearing. This is a phenomenon called yo-yo dieting, with people who have been on and off their diets, but they can't seem to gain any benefits from the diets that they adapt. If a diet isn't sustainable, then you will gain weight back as you get off it. Your metabolic rate takes a major blow by doing this.

The more suitable advice for people with autoimmune problems is that, no matter what, they should prioritize getting healthy from the inside. Even if there is no significant weight loss, they will effectively get to deal with joint aches or thyroid issues that are associated with autoimmune diseases.

The best way to adopt healthier eating habits is to simply start with changing one thing at a time. Major changes are disruptive for our bodies and are difficult to maintain.

It is almost impossible to gauge the amount of lectins in food items, but you can always check for the list of ingredients on the label. There are also many types of lectins, and they all have different functions. We must remember that the majority of studies on lectins are actually based on lectins in isolated form. That is where many of their negative effects are identified and broadcasted as a "toxin" to human health. The studies may reveal a different result if lectins were studied in the food form, the way we consume them. Human trials on the negative effects of lectins haven't been done yet. The claim that the lectins are really that destructive is dubious at best.

Nutritional science is truly very complicated. Facts are always changing. It is truly difficult to navigate to the actual truth when so much misinformation flows through channels that we should typically trust. Some experts have often called out nutrition science to be totally unreliable. They have stated that the relationship between disease and diet can also be classified as fiction ("The U.S. Dietary Guidelines: A Scientific Fraud | RealClearScience," 2019)[16].

Misinformation on such a topic can actually be harmful. That is not to say that there hasn't been any major progress. Many notable discoveries are made in this field. Many diseases have been correctly identified. Their causes are accurately traced back to the components of the diet we consume. Whether their absence or excess was the issue was then accurately established. However, revealing discoveries began to fade as nutrition science advanced.

The trouble also is the core belief, which is that chronic diseases are related to the diet of a person. The investigation of facts related to diet and disease are, for the most part, downright untrustworthy. They are often based on questionnaires and memory. Both methods have a very high chance of human error.

One study seems to suggest one thing about a certain food while the other claims that food is essentially a toxin. People who are genuinely interested in fitness and health are stuck in the middle. One reason why it is so confusing is that nutrition science is in the early stages of developments. It is quite young compared to other major science fields. People are more interested in the field of disease treatment, not in prevention. The former is where most of the researchers prefer to study. The studies that are often done on health topics are based on observations rather than concrete experimentation. It is not like your experiment can yield results right away. What we eat doesn't affect us on the spot or even after a limited time. It depends from person to person.

Food is rarely the main cause of diseases. It can be, however, a trigger for them. Whole categories of food should not be swept aside with one brush. Take shellfish, for example. They can cause a severe allergic reaction in somebody while they are perfectly nutritious for anybody else. A little example proves that food items should not be readily classified as toxic and harmful. It is a lot more complicated than that.

How we prepare and consume food plays a major role in the effects it has on our body. Take grains as an example. Highly processed grains are a major food that plays a role in excessive weight gain. It also causes inflammation and other diseases linked to it. However, the grains that are normally processed are classified as extremely beneficial to our health. These grains include wheat berries, quinoa, etc.

Theories Around Lectins

Some experts believe that lectins are also behind urinary tract infections.

There are also studies linking high lectin consumption with a growth rate of anemia. In developing countries, the abundant amount of lectin consumption could be leading people to develop anemia.

The top ten allergens including dairy, egg, peanuts, tree nuts, wheat, shellfish, fish, and soy all contain lectins in excessive amounts. It is a hypothesis among some experts that lectins are the root cause of many human health issues.

Information About Lectins

There are many different types of lectins present. Not all of them are dangerous toward human health. Only a few types are dangerous to humans, but that happens only under special circumstances.

Denmark is a country that has one of the lowest death rates in the world. During World War I, the Danish people were given food portions that mainly consisted of lectin-based items such as grains, potatoes, and beans. As one can ascertain, during war times, there is a shortage in terms of luxury foods especially the animal and fat based ones. So the people were not given these during the time of World War I. The huge lectin-based diet the Danes went on hasn't seemed to affect them badly at all.

Lectins in red kidney beans are known to be very harmful. Red kidney beans contain a high amount of phytohaemagglutinin. It is a very dangerous lectin and proven to be harmful to the digestive tract. This is the only lectin that has been singled out as the cause of some kind of harm for human health. That is why kidney beans are not to be eaten raw. The dried kidney bean cooked in a slow cooker is also not recommended as the temperature in there is not enough to deactivate the lectin activity.

Ricin is a deadly lectin. It is found in the castor bean plant's seeds. Castor bean plant is shrub-like with long-stemmed leaves.

There is ongoing research about the benefits of lectin found in mistletoe. There is some evidence that they restrict the growth of tumor cells (žarković et al., 1998)[17].

Our intake of these proteins serves a purpose. The healthiest of people who have lived the longest in the world have most of their diets based around plants. These diets often have lectins in abundance.

Just like water and sunlight are beneficial but can also cause harm to humans in one way or another, the same case applies to lectins.

There are a very large number of food items that contain lectin. They have a lot of nutritional value and functions to perform in our bodies. Some evidence is present that even suggests that they are helpful against cancer. (De Mejía & Prisecaru, 2005)[18]

Experts believe that studies which show that lectins are harmful to the human digestive tract, are stating facts in terms of lectins, taken in isolation. When they are taken in the context of food, the fact that they are so harmful doesn't apply anymore.

Common Food Toxins

There is an abundant amount of toxins that exist naturally. It is impossible to avoid them as they are present in so many common food items that we cannot afford to cut from our diet. We criticize the normal food products on their potential toxicity, but if we start inspecting the actual toxins, then we will be left with only a handful of foods to eat. All the trendy, healthy food that everybody sings praises about will be thrown out. So many reasons and facts against them will pop up because they contain these toxic substances. The crux is to not fret over every little nutritional fact of the meals you consume unless you are allergic or intolerant to some things. It is good to be interested in information about food, but you must be careful of the so-called truth behind it. Nutritional science can be misleading. You mustn't rely on it so much other than its proven discoveries.

Selenium Poisoning

Brazil nuts contain the highest concentration of this powerful antioxidant. As little as 4 of them could lead to toxicity from it. The toxic poisoning from it could lead to hair loss, fatigue, and neuropathy.

Mercury Poisoning

The common water available to us contains a lot of mercury. The mercury in water is usually caused by plumes created by manufacturing and materials production industries. Mercury goes inside fish present in the sea. We have to take caution before consuming it these days. Fish was once the healthiest thing that you could eat. Many fish today exceed the FDA mercury limit of 1 ppm.

Amylase Inhibitors

They are naturally occurring inhibitors. Their function is that they hinder the alpha-amylase. Alpha-amylase is usually found in red and white beans, wheat, and rye. Foods that contain these inhibitors can cause allergic reactions.

Goitrogens

Some foods interfere with the activity of the thyroid gland and cause an imbalance in the uptake of iodine. Goitrogens are also found in plenty of vegetables, peanuts, soybeans, and strawberries.

Furocoumarins

They can cause DNA damage. It is because they have phototoxic and photomutagenic properties. They can also cause dermatitis. They are mostly present in citrus fruits.

Anti-Thiamine Compounds

They wipe out the vitamin B-1 from our body. The deficiency of this particular vitamin could lead to weight loss and weakness. It also leads to the development of a condition known as "beriberi." It is a disease that causes anorexia. They are mostly present in blueberries, red beets, crab, and fish.

Oxalates

Oxalates can bind to minerals and calcium. By doing that, they are made insoluble, and their deficiency occurs. Oxalates also play a role in kidney stone development. Almost 65 percent of kidney stones contain calcium oxalate. They are found in green vegetables, coffee, and tea. Almost all of the healthy vegetables seem to contain oxalate.

Chapter 17: An Alternative To A Lectin-Free Diet

Gathering information about a lectin-free diet is essential. Once you have collected the details, you have to decide whether to follow the diet or not. But, if you can't follow the diet right away, try focusing on the things that you can do for the time being. So, what can you do? Consider doing the following:

You can try ditching the grains, legumes, and soy. But, if you can't, make sure to dig in for information about their nutritional value. They are low in minerals and vitamins. Also, they contain phytates, so mineral absorption is blocked. So, why do you need to eat something that doesn't provide health benefits?

If you are in love with legumes and grains, you don't have to give up those for now. Instead, try giving up peanuts and wheat, at least. They contain high lectins, and you already know the health problems caused by wheat. Hence, keep them away from your diet.

Do experiments often. You must know your body. Take time to understand the issues that cause sickness to your body. For example, in lectin-free diet, you have to omit nightshades and dairy products. So, you can experiment to find whether they are the reasons for your sickness. If you have stomach problems, you might react fast to lectin-rich food such as nightshades and dairy. Try keeping away dairy and nightshades for some time and track the progress. And then, try adding them back, and see the changes. If you feel bad after adding them back to your diet, you must set them away for some time. When you do this, you will feel great about yourself and your well-being.

Don't look for processed food. Instead, cook your own food. This is pretty easy because you get to choose what you want to cook. Also, cooking increases the chance to digest food efficiently.

Listen to your body. Not listening to your body is not a good choice. Above all, you will not be able to lead a healthy life. You must have a hawk-eyed vision of the foods that affect your body. However, to find the foods that affect your body, you must do a few experiments. You must consume certain foods for a certain period and see how it affects your body.

This is pretty much about the things that you can do to control lectin consumption. But, if you are still uninterested in the lectin-free diet, what are the other options that you can consider? Let me give you an overview of an alternative diet that you can follow instead of lectin-free diet. But, a disclaimer before we get started. This diet might include certain foods that are restricted by a lectin-free diet, but this is pretty much an alternative to a lectin-free diet. Shall we get started?

Yes, it is the Mediterranean Diet. This is a proven and achievable diet that you can follow if you are looking for an alternatives to the lectin-free diet. If you compare other diets with the Mediterranean diet, you will understand that it is not a diet; it just promotes healthy eating habits. You will be provided with a structure to follow if you want to eliminate unhealthy foods from your life. If you're going to get away from processed products, considering the Mediterranean Diet can be the right choice. You have to prepare your meals while adding more vegetables to your diet.

As you might imagine, this diet includes the eating habits followed by people in the Mediterranean areas along with Southern Italy and Greece. This can be considered as the comeback of the traditional diet. According to research, the early 1960s were the time when there was the lowest rate of heart diseases and the highest rate of life expectancy. The reason was eating habits, i.e., Mediterranean Diet. After the introduction of the Mediterranean Diet, there has been a good amount of evidence on the improvements encountered by the dieters. And, it was stated that the rate of deaths related to heart disease reduced. For someone who is addicted to processed foods, this can be daunting. But, the only option is to get started, and everything will fall into the right place.

You don't have to change in a day or two. Start with small changes to your eating habits. Over time, you will be amazed when you look at the way you have progressed. If you try to focus on the significant hauls, things can become impossible down the line. Like we mentioned before, you must set realistic expectations to achieve something new. You don't have a set time, pick a habit, and start following it. Try shopping for new and healthy vegetables. You can roast vegetables rather than preparing a boring salad. Make it fun and exciting. The exciting thing is that if you have never wanted to change, you might not be reading this book. So, reading this itself is a step that you have taken towards a healthy lifestyle.

Let me share something, I don't usually wake up with a happy mood, and it challenges my productivity. So, I started finding tips to overcome this unhappy mood issue. And then, I came across a useful video that stated ten tips to start your day productively. Once I watched, was I determined to follow the ten tips? Well, no! I thought of incorporating one tip at a time. Luckily, I have incorporated two tips by now. And I already feel the change. So, you see. Don't try to do all at once as it will not work, and it's impractical. Instead, do one thing at a time.

That being said, I hope you will try to do the same with the new eating habit that I'm going to share below.

Now that you know what the Mediterranean Diet means, it is time to focus on the foods that you can eat like a Mediterranean Dieter. What are the foods that are recommended? The Mediterranean Diet includes vegetables, fruits, fish, tubers, shrimp, sardines, and other healthy oils. The main focus is to reduce the rate of heart disease and harmful cholesterol. If you are determined to follow the Mediterranean Diet, you must make sure to stick to a meal plan. However, you are not forced to avoid many foods, so that you will be able to follow it on a long-term basis.

You can follow this diet because it is convenient. You don't have to face a lot of issues; the only issue is that you have to cook. But, cooking is fun if you have all the ingredients needed. Also, there are numerous meal plans and recipes offered to Mediterranean dieters, so you will not have a hard time when you try to cook healthy food.

There are inspirational diet plans that you can try out if you do not know how to start this diet. Even when you are eating out, you will not have difficulties because veggie salads are available in almost all the restaurants.

While eating healthy, you will be able to save time and money if you consider the Mediterranean Diet. You don't have to do quick shopping and waste money because you are in a rush. As you are required to cook your meal, you have to go shopping and keep things stored. If this becomes a practice, you will be able to save time and money.

Of course, you will not have hunger issues because this diet includes the necessary foods to satiate your hunger. In fact, olive oil can satiate your hunger, and you will be using it once you opt for the Mediterranean Diet.

Another good thing about the Mediterranean Diet is that it emphasizes exercise, too. So, this is more like a new lifestyle rather than a diet. But, you don't have to go to the extreme in exercising. Instead, you can walk often, or engage in any other exercise that you will continuously do. Try to add moderate-intensity exercise twice a week. This is not only about what you eat, but also about how you eat and how you live. You must take care of your body if you want to live healthily. When you follow this diet, you will not feel restricted. You will enjoy it because it really is enjoyable!

As I said, there are no strict rules if you are following the Mediterranean Diet. You have the option to give up dairy products if you are a vegetarian. Or if you are focused on a low-sodium diet, you can add spices and herbs while ignoring salt. Or for a person who's concerned about gluten, you can pick the things that are gluten-free.

Additional points about the Mediterranean Diet:

For someone who is looking forward to a meaningful lifestyle change, the Mediterranean Diet is the right option. You don't have to restrict anything, in particular, can try new recipes, and lead a happy, energetic life. Also, you can save money because you will not purchase whatever you see, as most eye-catching things are processed. And processed food is a big NO in Mediterranean Diet. Finally, you can keep learning the diet because there are many sources to get reliable and useful information. Based on the research, this diet has been proven to be one of the best diets.

This diet helps to improve heart health and the life expectancy. As per studies, it has displayed better results by lowering the rate of heart disease, cholesterol, blood pressure, diabetes, chronic disease, and cancers.

Also, it is no wonder healthy foods, exercise, and positive mindset are the ingredients for a healthy life. This diet is enjoyable and flexible, so most people are ready to follow it without a second thought. Even for someone who doesn't follow the diet 100%, there will be many health benefits because of healthy eating habits and proper exercises.

That's pretty much it about the Mediterranean Diet!

But, there are specific characteristics that most healthy diets rely on. Let's check out some of them:

Low glycemic. Most diets focus on low sugar, including refined carbohydrates.

More fruits and vegetables. Include more fruits and vegetables. But, it is better if there are many varieties and deeper colors. The high level of phytonutrients has the power to fight against many diseases.

Less or no pesticides. Almost all the diets recommend consuming foods that are fresh and healthy rather than the ones that contain antibiotics, pesticides, hormones, and much more. But, sometimes, it can be hard to find such foods, so you have to lower the intake.

No chemicals. Most diets strictly avoid dyes, artificial sweeteners, MSG, additives, preservatives, and other chemicals that are harmful to your body. It can be pretty tough to avoid artificial sweeteners, but do you want to sacrifice your health?

Quality fat. This is considered by almost all the diets, and it is omega-3 fats. There are some other quality fats such as olive oil and avocados.

Protein intake. This is emphasized in specific diets because it is essential for muscle synthesis and appetite control.

Organic food. It is always recommended to add fresh and local foods to your diet. If you are eating animal products, make sure to ensure that they are grass-fed. And when you consider fish, look for low-toxin fish, for example, herring, anchovies, and sardines. It is much better to avoid small fish because they are likely to have high mercury content.

The final result will include these:

Don't ever undermine the glycemic load when you are following a diet. Try to be concerned about fats and proteins. Don't consume canola, corn, sunflower, and soybean oil as they contain high calories. But, you can always opt for coconut, omega-3 fats, and avocados.

Try to eat more fresh vegetables and fruits. It is much better to add two or three vegetables. But, now that you are aware of lectins, you may decide to try to keep away from the vegetables that contain high lectins.

Avoid dairy as much as possible. Or if you really want to take it, go for organic products.

Another must-avoid factor is gluten. Even if you are not sensitive to it, it is better to keep it away. There are gluten-free products, so try to buy those when you are shopping.

If you eat meat, you must make sure to keep it as a side dish, not the main. Add more vegetables to your plate even if you eat meat.

Try to keep yourself away from eating sugar as much as possible.

As we wrap up this section on the Mediterranean Diet, above all these diets, there is one important diet that you must know. What is it? The Mental Diet. Without the Mental Diet, you will not be able to follow any other diets successfully. Hence, I'll run you through some quick, insightful information about the Mental Diet.

You might open the fridge to find something to eat. Or you might exercise on and off. But, if you want to stay in control, you must be able to control what you think and what you do. You must have the liberty to let in positive thoughts while shooing away the negative thoughts. It is possible to avoid lectins and to reduce weight. Or you can consider following the Mediterranean Diet instead of a lectin-free diet. It all depends on the way you think and decide. Your mind matters; so does your mental health!

This is why it is essential to focus on the mind diet. You can control the negative thoughts. Either you can react or avoid. Or you can consider it feedback and work on it. You can think about the things that you must put in your head and the things that you must neglect. You can let your mind run the race till you go to bed, or you can choose to let it rest for some time. So, if you really want to keep your mind in good health, consider the Mental Diet. Once you focus on it, you will be able to reduce overthinking and restlessness. However, how does one follow this diet? Here are some suggestions:

You have the controller to your thoughts, so control them.

More often, ask whether your thoughts are sensible and useful. Check whether they can help your personality.

Accept the fact that thoughts are selectable and you are the one who selects your thoughts. Even though thinking is automatic, with awareness, you can decide what to think and what not to. Also, self-discipline will help you to avoid unnecessary thoughts.

Make sure to avoid the thoughts that create unhappiness, strain, and stress. Of course, you cannot do this overnight. So, if you fail once, don't worry. Try frequently, and you will succeed. You will enhance this skill over time.

The mental diet must avoid anger, envy, and resentment.

The thoughts related to the fear of future and the past must be kept aside as much as possible. Even though it can be hard to at the beginning, you will get better over time with practice.

Through mental diet, you will be able to reduce mental noise and focus on inner peace.

However, without the significant tool of concentration, you cannot achieve success in the mental diet. Hence, try to improve your concentration, and it will eventually support inner strength and mental health.

This is going to be helpful when you follow the lectin-free diet or Mediterranean Diet because you can think straight.

Chapter 18: What Is The Ultimate Nutrition-Based Diet Plan?

Reasons To Stick To A Diet Plan

Everyone should eat a balanced diet and adopt a healthy lifestyle in order to enjoy good health. Good nutrition is extremely important for anybody's well-being. Its benefits go beyond just maintaining a healthy weight.

A diet plan ensures that the body gets all of the nutrients that it requires. Following a diet plan helps boost the immune system. Some more of its advantages are listed below.

- It prevents common diseases like cold and flu.
- It helps prevent heart diseases.
- It lowers high cholesterol and high blood pressure.
- It increases the ability to recover from illnesses.
- Good nutrition also lessens the risk of diabetes and some forms of cancers.
- Osteoporosis develops at an old age when bones and body become weak. Ensuring your nutrition needs are met lowers the risk of developing osteoporosis.
- Having good nutrition also means high energy levels throughout your day.

Good Nutrition

So we know the importance of good nutrition, but what is the meaning of the term good nutrition?

Good nutrition means that all the essential nutrients (i.e., proteins, minerals, and vitamins) are included in our diet. Our ideal meals should be packed with nutrients, but not with calories.

Here are some tips to ensure good nutrition:

- Good nutrition involves all kinds of foods groups (i.e., fruits, grains, and vegetables).
- Fruits and vegetables of all types should be included in our diet. Every fruit and vegetable has its own nutritional value and benefit. They are uniquely laden with different vitamins and fiber. Those substances are essential for our well-being. Make sure there is plenty of color in your daily food.
- Whole grain is the most beneficial of all other types of grains. At least half of your cereals, bread, and pasta should be made from whole grain. Whole grain is a very important component that should not be overlooked in your diet if you are looking to develop better health.
- Lean meats are cuts of meats that have fewer calories but a good amount of protein compared to the other cuts. Lean cuts of meat are healthier. We should not only rely on traditional sources of meat for our protein needs. Tofu, beans, and fish are very healthy alternatives to the meats. One could turn to these if they are wary of the disadvantages of meat.
- Try eating meals that have a sizable amount of calcium and iron content.

Portion-Control Diet

Portion control, in simple terms, is managing how many calories we are accepting at each meal.

It lets us have a handle on our diet so that we eat only the quantity that we actually need. We need portion control for all food groups such as vegetables, dairy, protein, grains, and fruits. Too much and too little of anything is unhealthy for us. Non-starchy vegetables are the food group which we don't have to worry much about, even if we consume a lot more than we actually need.

If we were served a plate of food that is bigger than usual, then we would end up eating much more than usual as well. A review of a study found out that large plates of food can increase the tendency to intake more than our average intake (Benton, 2015)[19].

Here are some tips for portion control:

- Swap out your meat portion with more vegetables.
- Use mobile apps to track your portions.
- Use food scales and other measures to help get an accurate idea of the portions you are eating.

The number of calories you consume depends on the lifestyle you lead. The intake of calories must align to how many you can utilize during the day. If there is an imbalance between those two quantities, then it would be bad for your health. If you consume more calories than you use, then you would end up gaining weight. If you consume less than the calories you require, then you will lose weight.

The recommended calorie intake for men is around 2,500 calories per day, and for women, the amount is 2,000 calories per day.

Portionwise Nutrition Content

Starchy carbohydrates are wheat, pasta, rice, cereals, bread, and potatoes. These ingredients should make up just over one-third portion of the food we eat. A healthier option is the wholegrain version of these food items. One starchy food item should be present with each of our meal. It's a common misconception that they are fattening, but it's mostly the fat we add on them. The fats we cook or serve them in adds into calorie count. This includes oil on chips or sauces on pasta.

The daily amount of fruit and vegetable recommended is five portions of a variety of fruit and vegetable. Smoothies and fruit juices don't count for a lot of portions. If you had one smoothie and two fruit juices, then it would amount to only one portion.

Fish should be included in our daily diet. At least two portions of fish should be eaten per week. Oily fish is especially helpful in reducing the risk of heart diseases.

Fats are also essential in a moderate amount in our diet. There are two types of fats: saturated fats and unsaturated fats.

The excessive amount of saturated fats can put you at risk of a cholesterol problem.

The recommended amount of saturated fat is 30 grams per day for a man and 20 grams for a woman.

We all know that if our diet contains unhealthy amounts of sugar, it can only spell bad things for our overall health and well-being. Too much sugar consumption can put us at risk of tooth decay and obesity. We can check the food labels to get an idea about the quantity of sugar in the foods we are going to consume. If it contains more than 22.5 g per 100 g of food, then that means the food is high in sugar. If it contains less than five g per 100 g, then it means the food is low in sugar.

Cut down salt, as much as you can, from your daily meals. If you have an uncontrolled amount of salt in your daily diet, then it can develop into a risk of high blood pressure in your body. About six g of salt a day is the recommended amount, and that is equal to a teaspoon. More than 1.5g per one hundred grams means that the food item has a high salt content.

Lectins (The Plant Paradox)

- All types of grains (whole wheat)
- Legumes, beans (soy)
- Nuts (almonds)
- Fruits and vegetables (tomatoes, eggplants, peppers, and potatoes)

The items in brackets are the most important one in the food group that is mentioned. As one can ascertain, it doesn't leave much choice of food for us.

The book has a selling point as it promises cures to ailments that are very common and prevalent among the people. Now, they find that some tweaks to their diet can let them break free of these troubling experiences. Then, the people are sure to grab this book, seeking these miraculous findings and claims made by its author. The author claims that lectins are mostly behind the common ailments. They include digestive issues, brain fog, lack of energy, adult acne, aching joints, and cravings.

Here are some of the diseases listed by author, that according to him were fixed in patients, when they followed the lectin-free diet protocol. These diseases include many autoimmune diseases, certain types of cancers, heart diseases, and weight problems. Some neurological problems also seemed to be helped by it such as Parkinson's and dementia. All these findings are very extraordinary. If only they were true and in reality, lectins were the main cause, as claimed by the author. These types of findings demand a lot of scientific evidence to back them. For them to be accepted as facts, the majority of scientists and experts must agree on it. The topic should also go through rigorous testing and substantial studies carried out by notable experts of the field.

The book contains facts that have no literature backing. The references are provided to support the facts, but it is mostly unrelated or inadequate. So to blindly put faith in this book and its "facts" is not recommended.

His approved list of food is very hard to find, and as a diet, it is not easy to maintain. For example, some of the items one would require are only pasture-raised poultry and grass-fed beef, non-grain energy bars, and noodles. It is kind of a wonder where the patients of the author get their required calories from.

The book fails to convince that lectins are an unhealthy or unsafe food group. There are not enough arguments to prove the theories made against lectins.

Good nutrition is very important to lead a healthy life. A lot of people are always in pursuit of facts and information that could help them make better choices in health-related matters. They deserve good information on essential food items.

The Overall Best Diet For A Person

The diet that is best highly varies from person to person. It is wrong to believe that a diet that lists some benefits will happen for each person that adapts it. There are a number of factors that affect one's response to a certain type of food. It is naive to believe that a diet plan that worked for someone will have the same exact results for you, as well.

The benefits of some diets are highly generalized, and that ends up causing more harm than good. The biggest factor that studies have found is the genetic composition of the individual. It is the biggest factor in determining the response of a diet for any individual ("Your best diet might depend on your genetics," 2019)[20].

The research found out that the effects of the type depended on the origin of each mice. This phenomenon could also be translated to humans.

So that means the optimal diet for each is also vastly different from each other. Most recommendations are based on the average responses from different people. So there is no way to tell if these recommendations will work for someone or not.

This line of research is paving the way for a genetic test. This could lead to the discovery of who will benefit and who will have the harmful effects of the certain types of diets. The researchers are working on the identification of genes and biological mechanisms that play a major role in our response to our diets.

Concerns Regarding Lectins In Diets

Those people who are following raw plant-based diets should be concerned about lectins. Health problems are caused when the lectin-containing food doesn't undergo any of the traditional processes that it is supposed to go through before consumption. These techniques are important, and some of them are as below:

- Soaking
- Pressure cooking
- Sprouting
- Sour leavening
- Slow cooking
- Curing
- Pickling
- Water swapping

There is also a long food history to go with lectin-rich foods. The argument that they should not be consumed at all is gravely misguided. The preparation is a big factor in consuming any sort of food. There is a long history which has essentially put together a roadmap for us to consume these items safely.

There are people who are extremely sensitive to lectin. The reasons are mostly genetic. The conditions they suffer from are sometimes could be directly caused by lectin or aggravated by lectins. People with these conditions are told to be wary of legumes also. It is possible that beans and legumes cause them problems, but lectins may not be the real culprit. There are other complex compounds present in these food items which may be causing them all the trouble.

In some conditions, our bodies are unable to handle lectins and may possibly invite on its negative effects. Some of the main diseases listed as a result of lectins are diabetes, ulcers, and rheumatoid arthritis. So the main question here is that since lectin containing foods are so traditional and common, why are most of us free from these types of horrible diseases?

Some chronic diseases can also alter the cells of the intestine. The alteration may be such that the usually harmless lectins suddenly pose a threat now to the health. Wheat is damaging for someone with the symptoms of rheumatoid arthritis. Peanuts have a negative effect on colon cancer and IBD syndromes. These harms are avoided successfully by the carbohydrates that we obtain from dietary fibers.

The biology behind it is that our cells are covered by glycoconjugates. A fine screen of sialic acid molecules is also present, which serves as a protection for our cells. This whole system means we are safe from any harmful effects of lectins. However, the enzyme neuraminidase could get rid of the sialic acid molecules responsible for protecting our cells. This enzyme is present in several small microorganisms responsible for making us sick such as influenza viruses and streptococci. Diabetes and arthritis also tend to happen post infections. The microorganisms in our body provide ways for lectin to carry out its harmful activities. The age-old lore of fasting during a fever makes sense now.

So all in all people who are suffering from any mild or chronic infections and on a raw plant-based diet should be wary of the negative side effects of lectins. They should avoid lectins until healing occurs. The difference that you have to understand is that lectin-based food was probably not the cause. But now a special circumstance has developed where they are potentially being troublesome. If the case is more severe and you truly think that these nutrients are the main cause of problems, then you should consult a doctor to guide you.

Some people with severe gastrointestinal issues may be aided if they reduce the lectins from their diets. Going lectin free may help them in issues such as diarrhea and also help them increase nutrient absorption. If you do suffer from inflammation, then it is better that you see a nutritionist for this issue. They will recommend a proper diet plan for you. Their diet plan will ensure that you get all the proper nutrients as well. If you follow a lectin-free diet without any proper consultation, then it may lead to an imbalance in your nutrition needs.

Conclusion

When there is a myriad of choices, no wonder you might get carried away. Yes, it is the same with diet programs. As there are so many diet fads, you might be confused about the reliability. It will be difficult to find the right diet program or to differentiate the right one from rest of the programs. Even though people say the lectin-free diet is excellent and it's helpful, you might not believe it right away.

And, it is evident that you might doubt because of the countless number of diet fads. Thorough research about lectins can further help in understanding whether a lectin-free diet would work right for you or not.

In the final analysis, we conclude that lectins are safe food components for the majority of the population. They are safe to consume. Many reliable authorities even consider it a bad idea to eliminate lectins from your diet. They are of the opinion that your general well-being could suffer if you cut off the extensive variety of food items that contain lectins. There are many reasons to believe that the lectin-free diet with all its groundbreaking claims should be taken with a grain of salt.

- The earth-shattering claims are the first sign of unreliability. They are big claims with a little foundation.

- The list of common food it cuts off from our diet is extensive.

- How can one diet affect everybody? It is not possible. People are vastly different, and their bodies are different, as well. Some are old, and some are young; some are strong, while others are not. One diet for all seems like a long shot.

Once you understand the procedures on how it affects your body, you will be able to manage your diet accordingly. No matter what people say, you must always do your homework before you decide to follow a diet. You must make sure to read as much as possible. Also, it is wise enough to understand the pros and cons related to the diet. Specific diet programs don't suit certain people, so it is in your hands to do the needful research. Ultimately, the decision is yours, so make it for yourself!

You must never hop on to something just because it is popular. Most popular things aren't as good as they sound. Hence, it is crucial to be careful when you are opting for a diet program. If you are planning to follow the lectin-free diet, you have been covered with the basics and the essentials. It is advisable for you to keep searching more about the diet. Educating yourself is never time wasted.

I have included a lot of information that every beginner lectin-free dieter might need. But, you must ensure that you read and understand everything that is mentioned in this book.

I hope this book accommodated your needs.

Cheers to a healthy life!

Part 2

What Are Lectins?

Plants are stuck in the ground and can't escape or hide like animals but they can fight back using chemistry, in part by using poisons they create. Lectin are proteins with an unknown purpose mostly found in the seed but Dr. Gundry's insight is that Lectins are poisons designed to basically kill anything eating them to ensure the sprouting of the plant's seedlings. Since we're much larger than plants anticipated we can endure much larger quantities of lectins but that simply means they will cause inflammation and chronic health issues years or decades down the line rather than killing us outright. The worst part is that we get so used to eating foods with lectin that we don't connect the dots until it's too late.

What Is The Lectin Free Diet?

-
Plants are living beings too and don't want to be eaten; roses have thorns and nettles have poisoned barbs that cause an itchy rash. When a plant is attacked or eaten it activates self-defense mechanisms, creating various toxins that are meant to make it taste unpleasant or otherwise repel the animal. These toxins include lectins, which accumulate in the plant and get ingested by a human if the plant ends up in the human food chain. This notion that we might be eating plants that are slowly poisoning us through lectins is what inspired the creation of Lectin Free Diet.

What's The Evidence On Lectins?

So far very little actual research has taken place to investigate lectins but we do know that Rhesus monkeys given peanut oil will develop atherosclerosis and that lectins are actually classified as anti-nutrients since they can block the absorption of other nutrients. We do have plenty of anecdotal evidence, such as that Italians refused to eat tomatoes for 200 years after Columbus brought them home since they didn't have a resistance to its lectin, and even then always peeled and de-seeded the tomatoes, which is where most of the lectin is found. They did the same with peppers, and Italians never jar or serve them with peels or seeds.

One oft-maligned lectin that's been stirring headlines and gut linings in recent years is gluten, a wheat protein used as a thickener in all sorts of foods. Gluten is normally tied to carbohydrates inside the grain but it's the industrial practice of isolating and adding it to foods (ice cream)to increase their volume some 80 years ago that's just now starting to cause problems. Note how long it took for gluten to take effect and apply that to any person – we can be eating a bean or legume for several decades before some chronic health problem appears and we'd never suspect this tiny bean is poisoning us.

Are Lectins Harmful to Your Gut?

Every person will react to lectins in a different way but there is always some kind of reaction. Lectins can aggravate existing gut conditions but a healthy person can often ignore any discomfort or tiny signs of inflammation caused by lectins. Many plants contain lectins, potentially causing inflammation, gut problems, brain fog and other chronic symptoms if ingested in large enough doses. Just like with any other substance, lectin poisoning has to do with dosage, chronic exposure and the overall strength of the immune system that goes into inflammation overdrive trying to fight off lectins, causing autoimmune disease. Gut lining in the human body is saturated with all sorts of bacteria that actually cause us to crave certain foods and it seems the carbohydrates that come with lectins are also to blame for the disruption of these bacteria that leads to Irritable Bowel Syndrome and Crohn's disease, among other things.

What About Going Lectin-Free?

Going lectin-free might be impossible, might not have any positive effects and even cause us so much trouble that our quality of life degrades in other ways. We mentioned lectins are bound to carbohydrates but it turns out lectin-rich plants are also an important source of phytonutrients, such as minerals, vitamins, and dietary fiber. Lectins are a part of the package and there doesn't seem to be a way to completely eliminate them. However, those who have chronic bowel problems or autoimmune diseases might try looking at how much lectin they're ingesting and eliminate at least a small portion to see what happens.

The lectin avoidance can help with:
- Irritable Bowel Syndrome
- Irritable Bowel Disease
- Brain fog
- Histamine intolerance
- Chronic fatigue and Fibromyalgia

Foods to Eat

- Pasture-raised meats
- Fish and Seafood
- A2 milk (Southern European cow's milk, goat's milk, and buffalo milk)
- Unsweetened coconut milk
- Almond flour
- Coconut flour
- Leafy, green vegetables (Kale, Collard Greens, Turnip Greens, Swiss Chard, Spinach, Mustard Greens, Rapini (Broccoli Rabe), Chinese cabbage, napa cabbage, Red and Green Leaf

and Romaine Lettuce, Watercress, Arugula, Turnip root; greens)
- Cruciferous vegetables (Broccoli, Cauliflower, Brussels sprouts, Horseradish, Cabbage, Daikon, Bok Choy, Rutabaga (swede), Kohlrabi, Savoy cabbage)
- Green beans
- Snow peas
- Green peas (occasionally)
- **Asparagus**
- **Garlic**
- **Onion**
- **Celery**
- **Mushrooms**
- Sweet potatoes
- **Yucca**
- **Avocado**
- **Olives**
- Extra virgin olive oil
- All spices and herbs
- Eggs free-range or Omega3
- Onion and garlic powder
- Seaweed/sea vegetables
- Raw honey
- Citrus fruits, berries, and pineapple are the recommended fructose-containing foods
- **Vinegars**
- Stevia sweetener

Foods to Avoid

- Peppers
- **Tomatoes**

- **Aubergines**
- **Carrots**
- Legumes - Beans, Peas, Lentils, Pea, Chickpea, Soybean, Peanuts
- **Squash**
- Nightshade vegetables - Eggplant, Potatoes, Okra, Tomatillos
- Cayenne pepper
- **Capsicum**
- Fruits, although in-season fruit is allowed in moderation
- Grains - Whole Grains: Amaranth, Barley, Brown Rice, Buckwheat, Bulgur (Cracked Wheat), Corn, Farro / Emmer, Grano, Millet, Oats, Oatmeal
- Popcorn, Whole Wheat Cereal Flakes, Muesli, Rolled Oats, Quinoa, Rye, Sorghum, Spelt, Teff, Wheat Berries, Wild Rice
- Peppers (bell peppers, chili peppers, paprika, tamales, tomatillos, pimentos etc)
- Meat from corn-fed animals
- A1 milk
- Refined Grains -Cornbread, Corn Tortillas, Couscous, Crackers, Flour Tortillas, Grits, Noodles, Spaghetti, Macaroni, Pitas, Pretzels, Ready-To-Eat Breakfast Cereals, White Bread, White Sandwich Buns and Rolls, White Rice

Risks of the Lectin-Free Diet

Lectin-free diet can be impossible for vegans, who rely on beans and legumes for protein, or people who can't afford anything other than fast food or packaged food products, all of which are seasoned with lectins in some shape or form. Lectin-free diet might also include having to explain to family and loved ones how come you're no longer eating beans, grains, and pasta. This may not sound like a big deal but we tend to socialize over the food we eat and suddenly dropping the majority of lectin-rich foods might cause those close to us to suddenly start treating us differently. That is if the dieter can even drop their favorite lectin delicacy from the diet since lectin-rich foods are also rich in carbohydrates that can cause an outright addiction to that sweet, sweet taste.

Benefits of the Lectin-Free Diet
Lectins act as irritants and inflammatory factors in the body, causing all sorts of annoyances and chronic problems. We tend to perceive the cause and the effect only when they happen close together, so going lectin-free might lead to suddenly solving a longstanding health problem that apparently has nothing to do with diets, such as eczema or joint pain. As with all diets, it's important to pay attention to how the body is reacting and always keep track of levels of pain and discomfort. There's no telling how lectins are impacting your life but if a lectin-free diet can help you live with a clear mind, clean skin and a settled tummy then it's done its job and provided all the benefits you could possibly need.

Vegetarian Recipes

Creamy Cauliflower Mashed

Time: 3 hours 10 minutes

Serve: 6

Ingredients:

- 1 cauliflower head, cut into florets
- 1/2 tsp garlic powder
- 1/2 tsp onion powder
- 4 oz coconut cream
- 4 tbsp ghee
- 8 oz vegetable broth
- 1/2 tsp pepper
- 1/2 tsp salt

Directions:

- Add vegetable stock and cauliflower florets into the slow cooker.
- Cover slow cooker with lid and cook on high for 3 hours.
- Mash the cauliflower using a masher or hand blender.
- Add remaining ingredients and stir until combined.
- Serve and enjoy.

Nutritional Value (Amount per Serving):

- Calories 137
- Fat 13.3 g

- Carbohydrates 4 g
- Sugar 1.9 g
- Protein 2.2 g
- Cholesterol 22 mg

Tasty Herbed Mushrooms

Time: 2 hours 10 minutes

Serve: 4

Ingredients:

- 1 lb mushrooms, stems trimmed
- 2 tbsp ghee
- 1/4 cup coconut milk
- 1/2 cup organic vegetable broth
- 1 bay leaf
- 2 tbsp thyme, chopped
- 4 garlic cloves, chopped
- Black pepper
- Sea salt

Directions:

- Add mushrooms, bay leaf, thyme, and garlic in a slow cooker.
- Add vegetable broth and season with pepper and salt. Stir well.
- Cover slow cooker and cook on low for 1 1/2 hours or until tender.
- Add coconut milk and ghee and cook for 30 minutes more.
- Serve and enjoy.

Nutritional Value (Amount per Serving):

- Calories 128
- Fat 10.6 g
- Carbohydrates 6.5 g

- Sugar 2.6 g
- Protein 4.8 g
- Cholesterol 16 mg

Easy Brussels Sprouts

Time: 2 hours 10 minutes

Serve: 8

Ingredients:

- 2 lbs fresh Brussels sprouts
- 3 tbsp dried cranberries
- 2 tbsp olive oil
- Pepper
- Salt

Directions:

- Add olive oil and Brussels sprouts to the slow cooker. Season with pepper and salt.
- Cover and cook on low for 2 hours. Add dried cranberries and mix well.
- Serve and enjoy.

Nutritional Value (Amount per Serving):

- Calories 80
- Fat 3.9 g
- Carbohydrates 10.6 g
- Sugar 2.5 g
- Protein 3.9 g
- Cholesterol 0 mg

Simple Dijon Brussels Sprouts

Time: 4 hours 10 minutes

Serve: 4

Ingredients:

- 1 lb Brussels sprouts, wash, trim, and cut in half
- 1/4 cup water
- 1 tbsp Dijon mustard
- 3 tbsp olive oil
- 1/4 tsp black pepper
- 1/4 tsp kosher salt

Directions:

- Add all ingredients to the slow cooker and mix well to combine.
- Cover slow cooker and cook on low for 4 hours.
- Stir well and serve.

Nutritional Value (Amount per Serving):

- Calories 142
- Fat 11.1 g
- Carbohydrates 10.6 g
- Sugar 2.5 g
- Protein 4.1 g
- Cholesterol 0 mg

Garlic Kale

Time: 4 hours 10 minutes

Serve: 6

Ingredients:

- 24 oz kale, cleaned and chopped
- 1 cup vegetable stock
- 1 tbsp brown mustard
- 5 garlic cloves, minced
- 1 large onion, chopped
- 1/2 tsp pepper
- 1/2 tsp salt

Directions:

- Add chopped kale to the slow cooker and place garlic and onion on top.
- Pour in the stock. Add mustard, pepper, and salt over the top.
- Cover slow cooker and cook on low for 4 hours.
- Stir well and serve.

Nutritional Value (Amount per Serving):

- Calories 72
- Fat 0.4 g
- Carbohydrates 16.1 g
- Sugar 1.4 g

- Protein 3.9 g
- Cholesterol 0 mg

Healthy Slow Cooker Spinach

Time: 4 hours 10 minutes

Serve: 6

Ingredients:

- 2 lbs spinach, chopped
- 1 1/2 cups coconut yogurt
- 2 tbsp fresh lemon juice
- 1/2 cup cilantro, chopped
- 2 tsp ground coriander
- 1 tbsp dried dill
- 4 green onions, chopped
- 3 tbsp olive oil
- 1/2 tsp black pepper
- 1 tsp salt

Directions:

- Add all ingredients except coconut yogurt into the slow cooker and stir well.
- Cover slow cooker and cook on low for 4 hours.
- Serve with yogurt and enjoy.

Nutritional Value (Amount per Serving):

- Calories 129
- Fat 8.7 g

- Carbohydrates 10.2 g
- Sugar 4.3 g
- Protein 5.7 g
- Cholesterol 0 mg

Easy Lemon Garlic Asparagus

Time: 2 hours 10 minutes

Serve: 8

Ingredients:

- 2 lbs asparagus, washed
- 1 lemon, sliced
- 1 tsp garlic salt
- 1 tsp basil
- 2 garlic cloves, minced
- 1/2 cup organic vegetable broth
- 4 tbsp lemon juice
- 1/2 tsp pepper
- 1/2 tsp salt

Directions:

- Place washed asparagus into the bottom of slow cooker.
- In a small bowl, mix together lemon juice, broth, garlic, basil, garlic salt, pepper, and salt.
- Pour bowl mixture over asparagus. Top with sliced lemons.
- Cover slow cooker and cook on low for 2 hours.
- Serve and enjoy.

Nutritional Value (Amount per Serving):

- Calories 30
- Fat 0.3 g
- Carbohydrates 5.2 g
- Sugar 2.4 g

- Protein 3 g
- Cholesterol 0 mg

Warm Millet

Time: 5 hours 5 minutes

Serve: 4

Ingredients:

- 1 cup millet
- 2 tbsp vanilla extract
- 3 tbsp coconut sugar
- 3 cups coconut milk
- 3 cups water

Directions:

- Add all ingredients to the slow cooker and stir well.
- Cover slow cooker and cook on low for 5 hours.
- Stir well and serve.

Nutritional Value (Amount per Serving):

- Calories 373
- Fat 11.1 g
- Carbohydrates 53.7 g
- Sugar 0.8 g
- Protein 7.3 g
- Cholesterol 0 mg

Cauliflower Coconut Curry

Time: 2 hours 10 minutes

Serve: 6

Ingredients:

- 4 cups cauliflower florets
- 1 1/2 tsp curry powder
- 2 cups coconut milk
- 2 tsp olive oil
- 2 garlic cloves, minced
- 1/2 tsp black pepper
- Sea salt

Directions:

- Add olive oil into the slow cooker. Add cauliflower florets into the slow cooker.
- Add remaining ingredients over the cauliflower florets.
- Cover slow cooker and cook on low for 1-2 hours.
- Serve and enjoy.

Nutritional Value (Amount per Serving):

- Calories 218
- Fat 20.8 g
- Carbohydrates 8.7 g
- Sugar 4.3 g
- Protein 3.3 g
- Cholesterol 0 mg

Lemon Thyme Carrots

Time: 3 hours 10 minutes

Serve: 4

Ingredients:

- 2 lbs carrots cut into julienne
- 1 tbsp lemon zest
- 1/4 cup lemon juice
- 1 tbsp fresh thyme, chopped
- 1/4 cup ghee
- 1 onion, diced
- Pepper
- Salt

Directions:

- Add onions and carrots to the slow cooker.
- In a small bowl, combine together ghee, lemon juice, lemon zest, and thyme.
- Pour bowl mixture over the carrots. Season with pepper and salt.
- Cover slow cooker and cook on high for 3 hours.
- Serve and enjoy.

Nutritional Value (Amount per Serving):

- Calories 223
- Fat 13 g
- Carbohydrates 26 g
- Sugar 12.7 g

- Protein 2.4 g
- Cholesterol 33 mg

Lemon Artichokes

Time: 5 hours 10 minutes

Serve: 2

Ingredients:

- 2 large artichokes
- 4 lemons, sliced
- 6 cups water
- For lemon sauce:
- 3 tbsp fresh lemon juice
- 1/3 cup ghee, melted
- 1/4 tsp salt

Directions:

- For lemon sauce in a small bowl, combine together all sauce ingredients and set aside.
- Cut top of artichokes then cut each artichoke in half. Scoop out the fuzzy center of artichokes.
- Place artichoke halves in the slow cooker then add lemon slices and water.
- Cover slow cooker and cook on low for 8 hours.
- Drain artichokes and serve with lemon sauce.

Nutritional Value (Amount per Serving):

- Calories 415
- Fat 34.8 g
- Carbohydrates 28.3 g
- Sugar 5 g

- Protein 6.9 g
- Cholesterol 87 mg

Creamy Sweet Potato Mashed

Time: 3 hours 10 minutes

Serve: 4

Ingredients:

- 3 lbs sweet potatoes, peeled and chopped
- 1 tbsp ghee
- 1 cup organic vegetable broth
- 1/4 tsp pepper
- 1 1/2 tsp salt

Directions:

- Add sweet potatoes, ghee, broth, pepper, and salt to the slow cooker.
- Cover slow cooker and cook on high for 3 hours.
- Mash potatoes using masher until smooth and creamy. Season with pepper and salt.
- Serve and enjoy.

Nutritional Value (Amount per Serving):

- Calories 439
- Fat 4.1 g
- Carbohydrates 95.2 g
- Sugar 1.9 g
- Protein 6.4 g
- Cholesterol 8 mg

Delicious Root Vegetables

Time: 5 hours 10 minutes

Serve: 6

Ingredients:

- 3 garlic cloves, chopped
- 2 cups carrots, peeled and diced
- 2 cups turnips, peel and diced
- 2 cups parsnips, peel and diced
- 1 onion, diced
- 1/4 cup water
- Pepper
- Salt

Directions:

- Add onion and garlic into the slow cooker.
- Add remaining vegetables over the onion. Season vegetables with pepper and salt.
- Add water and stir well. Cover slow cooker and cook on high for 5 hours.
- Serve and enjoy.

Nutritional Value (Amount per Serving):

- Calories 64
- Fat 0.2 g
- Carbohydrates 15.2 g
- Sugar 5.6 g
- Protein 1.3 g

- Cholesterol 0 mg

Mushroom Stroganoff

Time: 4 hours 20 minutes

Serve: 2

Ingredients:

- 1 lb mushrooms, sliced
- 1/4 cup coconut cream
- 3 garlic cloves, sliced
- 3 tsp paprika
- 1 stock cube
- 1 tbsp ghee
- 1 onion, diced

Directions:

- Heat ghee in a pan over medium heat.
- Add mushroom and onion and cook for 10 minutes.
- Transfer mushroom and onion mixture into the slow cooker.
- Add remaining ingredients to the slow cooker and mix well.
- Cover slow cooker and cook on high for 4 hours.
- Serve and enjoy.

Nutritional Value (Amount per Serving):

- Calories 219
- Fat 14.8 g
- Carbohydrates 18.6 g
- Sugar 7.6 g
- Protein 9.7 g
- Cholesterol 16 mg

Healthy Roasted Vegetables

Time: 3 hours 10 minutes

Serve: 2

Ingredients:

- 1/2 cauliflower head, chopped
- 1 parsnip, peeled and chopped
- 1/2 lb carrots, peeled and chopped
- 1/2 onion, sliced
- 1/2 tsp cumin
- 1 tbsp olive oil
- 1/2 tsp salt

Directions:

- Add all ingredients to the slow cooker and mix well.
- Cover slow cooker and cook on low for 3-4 hours or until vegetable are tender.
- Serve and enjoy.

Nutritional Value (Amount per Serving):

- Calories 193
- Fat 7.5 g
- Carbohydrates 31.1 g
- Sugar 12.2 g
- Protein 3.7 g
- Cholesterol 0 mg

Savory Sweet Potato Mash

Time: 4 hours 10 minutes

Serve: 5

Ingredients:

- 2 lbs sweet potatoes, peeled and diced
- 2 tbsp coconut cream
- 1/2 cup coconut milk
- 3 garlic cloves, minced
- 1 tbsp ghee
- Pepper
- Salt

Directions:

- Add sweet potatoes into the slow cooker and pour enough water to cover them.
- Add salt and stir well. Cover and cook on low for 4 hours.
- Heat ghee in a small pan over medium heat. Add garlic and sauté until lightly brown.
- Drain sweet potatoes in a colander and return to the slow cooker.
- Add garlic ghee over them, add coconut cream and coconut milk and mash until smooth.
- Season with pepper and salt.
- Serve and enjoy.

Nutritional Value (Amount per Serving):

- Calories 266

- Fat 5.5 g
- Carbohydrates 51.8 g
- Sugar 1.1 g
- Protein 3.2 g
- Cholesterol 7 mg

Parsnips Cauliflower Mash

Time: 3 hours 10 minutes

Serve: 6

Ingredients:

- 1 lb parsnips, peel and chopped
- 4 garlic cloves, roasted
- 4 oz coconut cream
- 2 tbsp ghee, melted
- 1 lb cauliflower, cut into florets
- Pepper
- Salt

Directions:

- Add melted ghee into the slow cooker then add parsnips and cauliflower and stir well.
- Cover slow cooker and cook on low for 3 hours.
- Add garlic cloves and coconut cream and stir well. Puree using an immersion blender until smooth and creamy.
- Season with pepper and salt.
- Serve and enjoy.

Nutritional Value (Amount per Serving):

- Calories 160
- Fat 9.1 g
- Carbohydrates 19.3 g
- Sugar 6.1 g
- Protein 3 g

- Cholesterol 11 mg

Roasted Herb Beets

Time: 6 hours 10 minutes

Serve: 8

Ingredients:

- 12 beets, peel and diced
- 1 tbsp fresh rosemary, minced
- 1 tbsp parsley, minced
- 1 tsp dried thyme
- 2 tbsp olive oil
- 4 garlic cloves, minced
- 1/2 tsp pepper
- 1/2 tsp salt

Directions:

- Add beets into the slow cooker. Add garlic, thyme, olive oil, 1/4 cup water, pepper, and salt.
- Stir well to mix. Cover slow cooker and cook on low for 6 hours.
- Garnish with parsley and serve.

Nutritional Value (Amount per Serving):

- Calories 100
- Fat 3.9 g
- Carbohydrates 15.9 g
- Sugar 12 g
- Protein 2.7 g
- Cholesterol 0 mg

Herbed Onion Mushrooms

Time: 4 hours 10 minutes

Serve: 10

Ingredients:

- 4 cups mushrooms, sliced
- 4 cups onions, sliced
- 1 garlic clove, minced
- 1/2 tsp thyme
- 1/2 tsp oregano
- 1/2 cup organic butter, sliced
- 1/2 tsp black pepper
- 1/2 tsp sea salt

Directions:

- Add mushrooms and onions into the slow cooker. Top with garlic, butter, and seasonings.
- Cover slow cooker and cook on high for 4 hours.
- Stir well and serve.

Nutritional Value (Amount per Serving):

- Calories 107
- Fat 9.4 g
- Carbohydrates 5.5 g
- Sugar 2.4 g
- Protein 1.5 g
- Cholesterol 24 mg

Simple Collard Greens

Time: 6 hours 10 minutes

Serve: 8

Ingredients:

- 1 lb collard greens, rinsed and remove tough stems
- 1 smoked turkey leg
- 2 cups organic chicken broth
- 1 cup onion, chopped
- 1/4 tsp pepper
- 1/2 tsp salt

Directions:

- Add collard greens and onion into the slow cooker and top with a turkey leg.
- Season with pepper and salt. Pour broth over the greens.
- Cover slow cooker and cook on low for 6 hours.
- Serve and enjoy.

Nutritional Value (Amount per Serving):

- Calories 45
- Fat 1.4 g
- Carbohydrates 4.9 g
- Sugar 0.9 g
- Protein 4.5 g
- Cholesterol 6 mg

Soup & Stew Recipes

Creamy Broccoli Cauliflower Soup

Time: 4 hours 20 minutes

Serve: 6

Ingredients:

- 12 oz broccoli florets
- 2 lbs cauliflower florets
- 1/4 cup coconut cream
- 2 green onions, chopped
- 1/4 tsp dried thyme
- 1 tsp garlic powder
- 1 tsp onion powder
- 2 cups vegetable stock
- 1/4 tsp pepper
- 1/2 tsp salt

Directions:

- Add cauliflower, green onions, thyme, garlic powder, onion powder, vegetable stock, pepper, and salt to the slow cooker.
- Cover slow cooker with lid and cook on high for 4 hours.
- Transfer slow cooker mixture into a blender and puree until smooth and creamy.

- Return cauliflower puree into the slow cooker. Stir in coconut cream and broccoli.
- Cover the slow cooker with lid and cook on high for 10 minutes. Season with pepper and salt.
- Stir well and serve.

Nutritional Value (Amount per Serving):

- Calories 87
- Fat 3.1 g
- Carbohydrates 13.8 g
- Sugar 5.6 g
- Protein 5 g
- Cholesterol 0 mg

Perfect Cauliflower Soup

Time: 8 hours 10 minutes

Serve: 2

Ingredients:

- 4 1/2 cups cauliflower florets
- 1 cup water
- 2 cups vegetable stock
- 1 tbsp olive oil
- 2 cups leeks
- 1 tsp salt

Directions:

- Add all ingredients except water into the slow cooker and stir well.
- Cover slow cooker with lid and cook on low for 8 hours.
- Puree the soup using an immersion blender until smooth. Add water until getting your desired consistency.
- Serve and enjoy.

Nutritional Value (Amount per Serving):

- Calories 176
- Fat 8.5 g
- Carbohydrates 25.5 g
- Sugar 9.9 g
- Protein 5.8 g
- Cholesterol 0 mg

Healthy Ginger Broccoli Soup

Time: 3 hours 10 minutes

Serve: 6

Ingredients:

- 8 cups broccoli florets
- 6 cups vegetable stock
- 1 tbsp olive oil
- 1 tsp turmeric
- 2 tbsp ginger, chopped
- 4 cups leeks, chopped
- 2 tbsp ghee
- 1/8 tsp black pepper
- 1 tsp salt

Directions:

- Heat pan over medium heat, and melt the ghee. Add leeks and cook for 8 minutes.
- Transfer the leeks to a slow cooker with remaining ingredients and stir well.
- Cover slow cooker and cook on low for 3 hours.
- Puree the soup using an immersion blender until smooth and creamy.
- Serve and enjoy.

Nutritional Value (Amount per Serving):

- Calories 153
- Fat 9.3 g

- Carbohydrates 20 g
- Sugar 6.4 g
- Protein 4.5 g
- Cholesterol 11 mg

Delicious Beef Chili

Time: 6 hours 15 minutes

Serve: 4

Ingredients:

- 1 lb grass-fed ground beef
- 1 tsp coconut aminos
- 1 tsp red wine vinegar
- 7.5 oz can sweet potato puree
- 1 oz pine nuts
- 1 cup vegetable stock
- 1/8 tsp cinnamon
- 1 tsp ground cumin
- 1 tbsp chili powder
- 1 celery rib, diced
- 1/2 onion, diced
- 2 garlic cloves, minced
- 1 tbsp olive oil
- Pepper
- Salt

Directions:

- Heat olive oil in a large pan over medium-high heat.
- Add ground beef and cook for 3-4 minutes. Transfer ground beef to the slow cooker.
- Turn heat to medium and add onion, garlic, and celery to the pan and sauté for 5 minutes or until softened.

- Add cinnamon, cumin, and chili powder and stir for 1 minute.
- Pour in the vegetable stock, scrape the bottom of the pan and transfer to the slow cooker.
- Add coconut aminos, vinegar, sweet potato puree, pine nuts, pepper, and salt to the slow cooker and stir well.
- Cover slow cooker with lid and cook on low for 6 hours.
- Serve and enjoy.

Nutritional Value (Amount per Serving):
- Calories 353
- Fat 20.4 g
- Carbohydrates 17.4 g
- Sugar 7.8 g
- Protein 25.9 g
- Cholesterol 75 mg

Creamy Mushroom Soup

Time: 4 hours 10 minutes

Serve: 4

Ingredients:

- 6 cups mushrooms, sliced
- 1 tsp dry dill
- 1 cup coconut milk
- 2 tsp dried thyme
- 4 cups vegetable stock
- 1/4 cup balsamic vinegar
- 2 garlic cloves, minced
- 1 medium onion, sliced
- 2 tbsp olive oil
- 1/2 tsp black pepper
- 1 tsp kosher salt

Directions:

- Heat olive oil in a large pan over high heat.
- Add garlic, onion, and mushrooms and sauté until mushrooms are tender.
- Add vinegar and simmer until vinegar reduced by half.
- Transfer mushroom mixture to slow cooker and add stock, thyme, pepper, and salt.
- Cover slow cooker and cook on low for 4 hours.
- Add coconut milk during last 15 minutes of cooking time and continue to cook for last 15 minutes.

- Transfer mixture to a blender and blend until smooth and creamy.
- Add dill and stir well.
- Serve and enjoy.

Nutritional Value (Amount per Serving):

- Calories 242
- Fat 22.2 g
- Carbohydrates 11.1 g
- Sugar 5.6 g
- Protein 5.2 g
- Cholesterol 0 mg

Beef Cabbage Soup

Time: 6 hours 10 minutes

Serve: 8

Ingredients:

- 1 lb grass-fed ground beef
- 2 bay leaf
- 1/2 tsp garlic powder
- 1 tbsp Italian seasoning
- 6 cups vegetable broth
- 1 lb cabbage, shredded
- 1 large onion, chopped
- 1 tbsp olive oil
- 1/4 tsp black pepper
- 1 tsp sea salt

Directions:

- Heat olive oil in a large pan over medium heat.
- Add onion and sauté for 10-15 minutes. Add ground beef and season with pepper and salt.
- Cook ground beef for 8-10 minutes or until browned.
- Meanwhile, add the remaining ingredients to the slow cooker.
- Once beef is browned, add the beef and onion mixture to the slow cooker. Stir well.
- Cover slow cooker and cook on low for 6 hours.
- Serve and enjoy.

Nutritional Value (Amount per Serving):

- Calories 172
- Fat 8.9 g
- Carbohydrates 6.1 g
- Sugar 3.3 g
- Protein 16.2 g
- Cholesterol 39 mg

Chicken Cabbage Soup

Time: 6 hours 10 minutes

Serve: 4

Ingredients:

- 3 lbs pastured chicken, cut into parts and trim excess fat
- 2 scallions, chopped
- 1 tbsp ginger, sliced
- 6 garlic cloves
- 1/2 medium onion, chopped
- 12 oz Napa cabbage, cut cabbage leaves into pieces
- Pepper
- Salt

Directions:

- Add chicken into the slow cooker. Add cabbage, onion, ginger, and garlic on top of chicken.
- Add 8 cups water, 1/4 teaspoon of pepper, and 1 tablespoon of salt.
- Cover slow cooker and cook on low for 6 hours.
- Add scallions and stir well. Season with pepper and salt to taste.
- Serve and enjoy.

Nutritional Value (Amount per Serving):

- Calories 544
- Fat 10.6 g
- Carbohydrates 6.2 g

- Sugar 1.9 g
- Protein 100.6 g
- Cholesterol 262 mg

Okra Beef Stew

Time: 4 hours 10 minutes

Serve: 2

Ingredients:

- 1 cup fresh okra, chopped
- 2 cups organic vegetable stock
- 1/4 tsp cinnamon
- 1/2 tsp black pepper
- 1 tsp cumin
- 2 garlic cloves, crushed
- 1 large onion, chopped
- 1 lb grass-fed beef, diced
- 1 tbsp olive oil
- Salt

Directions:

- Heat olive oil in a pan over medium heat.
- Add beef and cook from all sides until brown then transfer in the slow cooker.
- Add remaining ingredients into the slow cooker and stir well.
- Cover slow cooker and cook on low for 4 hours.
- Serve and enjoy.

Nutritional Value (Amount per Serving):

- Calories 537
- Fat 29.5 g
- Carbohydrates 15.7 g

- Sugar 6.9 g
- Protein 48.4 g
- Cholesterol 151 mg

Creamy Asparagus Soup

Time: 8 hours 10 minutes

Serve: 8

Ingredients:

- 2 lbs asparagus, wash and trim
- 1/2 cup coconut milk
- 5 cups water
- 1 cup onion, chopped
- Pepper
- Salt

Directions:

- Add asparagus, water, and onion into the slow cooker.
- Cover slow cooker and cook on low for 8 hours.
- Puree the soup using an immersion blender until smooth and creamy.
- Stir in coconut milk until combined. Season with pepper and salt.
- Serve and enjoy.

Nutritional Value (Amount per Serving):

- Calories 63
- Fat 3.7 g
- Carbohydrates 6.6 g
- Sugar 3.2 g
- Protein 3 g
- Cholesterol 0 mg

Mushroom Asparagus Soup

Time: 4 hours 10 minutes

Serve: 6

Ingredients:

- 1/2 lb mushrooms, sliced
- 1/2 lb asparagus, sliced into 1" pieces
- 2 tbsp olive oil
- 1/2 cup onion, chopped
- 1/4 tsp garlic salt
- 1 cup coconut milk
- 4 cups organic vegetable stock

Directions:

- Add asparagus, mushrooms, onion, olive oil, coconut milk, and stock in the slow cooker.
- Cover slow cooker and cook on high for 4 hours.
- Add garlic salt and stir well.
- Serve and enjoy.

Nutritional Value (Amount per Serving):

- Calories 162
- Fat 14.4 g
- Carbohydrates 7.9 g
- Sugar 5.1 g
- Protein 3.1 g
- Cholesterol 0 mg

Leek Sweet Potato Soup

Time: 4 hours 10 minutes

Serve: 4

Ingredients:

- 2 lbs sweet potatoes, peeled and chopped
- 1 tbsp ghee
- 1/2 tsp thyme
- 4 cups organic vegetable broth
- 4 leeks, sliced
- 1/4 tsp pepper
- 1 1/2 tsp garlic salt

Directions:

- Add all ingredients to the slow cooker and stir well.
- Cover slow cooker and cook on low for 4 hours.
- Puree the soup using an immersion blender until smooth and creamy.
- Serve and enjoy.

Nutritional Value (Amount per Serving):

- Calories 393
- Fat 5.2 g
- Carbohydrates 77.7 g
- Sugar 5.6 g
- Protein 9.9 g
- Cholesterol 8 mg

Salmon Coconut Stew

Time: 2 hours 10 minutes

Serve: 4

Ingredients:

- 8 oz wild-caught salmon
- 1/2 tsp coriander
- 1 tsp ginger, chopped
- 1 tbsp curry powder
- 1/2 small onion, diced
- 1/2 cup water
- 14 oz coconut milk
- 1/4 tsp pepper
- 1 1/2 tsp salt

Directions:

- Add all ingredients to the slow cooker and stir well.
- Cover slow cooker and cook on high for 2 hours.
- Serve and enjoy.

Nutritional Value (Amount per Serving):

- Calories 318
- Fat 26.4 g
- Carbohydrates 7.6 g
- Sugar 3.7 g
- Protein 15.9 g
- Cholesterol 31 mg

Chicken Mushroom Soup

Time: 3 hours 40 minutes

Serve: 4

Ingredients:

- 8 oz mushrooms, sliced
- 1/2 lb pastured chicken breasts, diced
- 2 celery stalks, chopped
- 2 carrots, chopped
- 1 onion, chopped
- 4 green onions, diced
- 2 cups water
- 4 cups organic chicken broth
- 1/2 tsp pepper
- 1 tsp salt

Directions:

- Add chicken, celery, carrot, onion, water, broth, pepper, and salt to the slow cooker. Stir well.
- Cover slow cooker and cook on high for 3 hours.
- Add green onions and mushrooms and stir well.
- Cover slow cooker again and cook for 30 minutes more.
- Stir well and serve.

Nutritional Value (Amount per Serving):

- Calories 189
- Fat 5.8 g
- Carbohydrates 9.9 g

- Sugar 4.8 g
- Protein 23.9 g
- Cholesterol 50 mg

Easy Carrot Soup

Time: 8 hours 10 minutes

Serve: 6

Ingredients:

- 8 medium carrots, peeled and chopped
- 1 cup coconut milk
- 3 cups organic vegetable broth
- 1 tsp curry powder
- 1 garlic clove, minced
- 1 onion, chopped
- 1/8 tsp allspice
- 1/4 tsp salt

Directions:

- Add carrots, broth, allspice, garlic, curry powder, onion, and salt into the slow cooker.
- Cover slow cooker and cook on low for 8 hours or until tender.
- Puree the soup using an immersion blender until smooth and creamy.
- Add coconut milk and stir well.
- Serve and enjoy.

Nutritional Value (Amount per Serving):

- Calories 154
- Fat 10.3 g
- Carbohydrates 12.8 g

- Sugar 6.5 g
- Protein 4.3 g
- Cholesterol 0 mg

Creamy Carrot Sweet Potato Soup

Time: 8 hours 10 minutes

Serve: 2

Ingredients:

- 1 lb sweet potatoes, peel and diced
- 1 medium carrot, diced
- 1 onion, diced
- 3 cups water
- 1/2 cinnamon stick
- 1/2 tbsp curry powder
- 1/2 tbsp ginger, grated
- Pepper
- Salt

Directions:

- Add all ingredients to the slow cooker and stir well.
- Cover slow cooker and cook on low for 8 hours.
- Discard cinnamon stick form slow cooker.
- Puree the soup using an immersion blender until smooth.
- Serve and enjoy.

Nutritional Value (Amount per Serving):

- Calories 312
- Fat 0.8 g
- Carbohydrates 73.3 g
- Sugar 5.1 g
- Protein 4.7 g

- Cholesterol 0 mg

Simple Chicken Vegetable Soup

Time: 6 hours 10 minutes

Serve: 2

Ingredients:

- 1 pastured chicken breast, skinless, boneless, and cut into cubes
- 3/8 tsp chicken bouillon cubes
- 1/2 celery stalk, chopped
- 1/2 carrots, peeled and diced
- 1 garlic clove, minced
- 1/4 onion, diced
- 14 oz organic chicken broth
- 1/8 tsp pepper
- 1/8 tsp thyme
- 1/4 tsp oregano
- Salt

Directions:

- Add all ingredients to the slow cooker and stir well.
- Cover slow cooker and cook on low for 6 hours.
- Serve and enjoy.

Nutritional Value (Amount per Serving):

- Calories 191
- Fat 4.1 g
- Carbohydrates 4.4 g
- Sugar 2 g

- Protein 32 g
- Cholesterol 73 mg

Avocado Chicken Soup

Time: 8 hours 10 minutes

Serve: 6

Ingredients:

- 1 lb pastured chicken breast
- 1 tbsp lime juice
- 1 tsp black pepper
- 1/4 tsp cumin
- 2 garlic cloves, minced
- 1 celery stalk, diced
- 3 green onion stalks, chopped
- 64 oz organic chicken broth
- 2 avocados, sliced
- 1 1/2 tsp salt

Directions:

- Add all ingredients except avocados into the slow cooker and stir well.
- Cover slow cooker and cook on low for 8 hours.
- Remove chicken from slow cooker and shred using a fork.
- Return shredded chicken into the slow cooker with sliced avocados and stir well.
- Serve immediately and enjoy.

Nutritional Value (Amount per Serving):

- Calories 274
- Fat 16.7 g

- Carbohydrates 7.6 g
- Sugar 1.3 g
- Protein 23.6 g
- Cholesterol 48 mg

Healthy Spinach Broccoli Soup

Time: 4 hours 40 minutes

Serve: 6

Ingredients:

- 2 1/2 cups broccoli florets
- 5 oz baby spinach
- 4 1/2 cups organic vegetable broth
- 3 garlic cloves, minced
- 1 cup onion, chopped
- 1/2 tsp black pepper
- 1 1/2 tsp salt

Directions:

- Add all ingredients except spinach into the slow cooker and stir well.
- Cover slow cooker and cook on high for 4 hours.
- Add spinach and cook for 30 minutes more.
- Puree the soup using an immersion blender until smooth.
- Serve and enjoy.

Nutritional Value (Amount per Serving):

- Calories 58
- Fat 1.3 g
- Carbohydrates 6.5 g
- Sugar 2.1 g
- Protein 5.7 g
- Cholesterol 0 mg

Creamy Garlic Asparagus Soup

Time: 8 hours 10 minutes

Serve: 4

Ingredients:

- 1 lb asparagus, ends trimmed and chopped
- 1 tsp lemon juice
- 1/2 cup coconut yogurt
- 3 cups organic vegetable stock
- 2 garlic cloves, minced
- 1 large onion, diced
- Pepper
- Salt

Directions:

- Add asparagus, stock, garlic, and onion to the slow cooker and stir well.
- Cover slow cooker and cook on low for 8 hours.
- Puree the soup using a blender until smooth and creamy.
- Stir in coconut yogurt and lemon juice. Season with pepper and salt.
- Serve and enjoy.

Nutritional Value (Amount per Serving):

- Calories 65
- Fat 0.7 g
- Carbohydrates 12.4 g
- Sugar 7.6 g

- Protein 3.5 g
- Cholesterol 0 mg

Cauliflower Asparagus Soup

Time: 6 hours 10 minutes

Serve: 2

Ingredients:

- 1 lb asparagus, cut into 1/2" pieces
- 3 cups organic vegetable broth
- 1 cup cauliflower, chopped
- 2 tbsp olive oil
- 1 large onion, chopped
- 1 lemon juice
- Pepper
- Salt

Directions:

- Heat olive oil in a pan over medium-high heat.
- Add onion and sauté until softened. Transfer onion to the slow cooker.
- Add remaining ingredients except for lemon juice into the slow cooker and stir well.
- Cover slow cooker and cook on low for 4-6 hours.
- Puree the soup using a blender until smooth and creamy.
- Stir in lemon juice and season with pepper and salt.
- Serve and enjoy.

Nutritional Value (Amount per Serving):

- Calories 266
- Fat 16.5 g

- Carbohydrates 19.9 g
- Sugar 9.7 g
- Protein 14.1 g
- Cholesterol 0 mg

Meat Recipes

Pork With Cabbage

Time: 8 hours 10 minutes

Serve: 6

Ingredients:

- 3 lbs pastured pork roast
- 1/2 cabbage head, chopped
- 1 cup water
- 1/3 cup liquid smoke
- 1 tbsp kosher salt

Directions:

- Rub pork with kosher salt and pour on liquid smoke. Place in slow cooker.
- Add water and cover slow cooker and cook on low for 8 hours.
- Remove pork from slow cooker during the last 1 hour of cooking and add cabbage in the bottom of slow cooker.
- Now place pork on top of the cabbage.
- Cover slow cooker and cook continue for remaining 1 hour.
- Shred the pork with a fork and serve.

Nutritional Value (Amount per Serving):

- Calories 484
- Fat 21.5 g

- Carbohydrates 3.5 g
- Sugar 1.9 g
- Protein 65.4 g
- Cholesterol 195 mg

Chicken With Garlicky Spinach

Time: 4 hours 35 minutes

Serve: 4

Ingredients:

- 4 pastured chicken thighs, trimmed
- 12 oz baby spinach
- 1 tbsp pine nuts, toasted
- 1 tbsp fresh lemon juice
- 1/4 cup raisins
- 1/4 cup water
- 1/2 tsp paprika
- 1 tsp olive oil
- 4 garlic cloves, sliced
- 1 onion, chopped
- Pepper
- Salt

Directions:

- Spray slow cooker from inside with cooking spray.
- Add onion, olive oil, and garlic in a microwave-safe bowl and microwave for 5 minutes or until softened.
- Transfer onion mixture to the slow cooker. Add water and stir well.
- Season chicken with pepper and salt and place in slow cooker.
- Cover slow cooker and cook on low for 4 hours.

- Transfer chicken to plate. Add spinach and stir until spinach is wilted. Add raisins and stir well.
- Return chicken to slow cooker. Cover and cook on high for about 20 minutes.
- Transfer chicken to plate. Stir pine nuts and lemon juice into spinach and season with pepper and salt.
- Serve chicken and spinach and enjoy.

Nutritional Value (Amount per Serving):

- Calories 366
- Fat 14 g
- Carbohydrates 14.4 g
- Sugar 7.1 g
- Protein 45.8 g
- Cholesterol 130 mg

Artichoke Spinach Chicken

Time: 3 hours 40 minutes

Serve: 4

Ingredients:

- 2 lbs pastured chicken breasts, skinless and boneless
- 3 oz baby spinach
- 1/2 cup dry white wine
- 1/2 cup organic chicken stock
- 1 lemon, cut into wedges
- 1 shallot, sliced
- 2 garlic cloves, smashed
- 1 1/2 cups can artichoke hearts, drained and sliced
- 1/2 tsp black pepper
- 3/4 tsp kosher salt

Directions:

- Season chicken with pepper and salt and place in slow cooker.
- Add artichoke, lemon wedges, shallot, and garlic.
- Pour in stock and wine. Cover slow cooker and cook on low for 3 1/2 hours.
- Transfer chicken to a dish. Add spinach to the slow cooker and stir with lemon and artichokes.
- Transfer spinach artichoke mixture to the chicken dish.
- Serve and enjoy.

Nutritional Value (Amount per Serving):

- Calories 487
- Fat 17.1 g
- Carbohydrates 7.2 g
- Sugar 0.9 g
- Protein 68 g
- Cholesterol 202 mg

Beef Chuck Roast

Time: 8 hours 20 minutes

Serve: 6

Ingredients:

- 2 lbs grass-fed beef chuck roast
- 1 tbsp balsamic vinegar
- 1/4 tsp thyme, chopped
- 1 bay leaf
- 1 cup dry red wine
- 2 garlic cloves, minced
- 1 celery stalk, chopped
- 1 large carrot, chopped
- 3 cups organic chicken broth
- 2 tbsp olive oil
- Pepper
- Salt

Directions:

- Season meat with pepper and salt.
- Heat olive oil in a pan over medium heat. Sear season meat on all side until lightly brown.
- Transfer meat to slow cooker. Add onion in a pan and cook until softened, about 8 minutes.
- Add celery and carrot and continue to stir for 5 minutes. Add garlic and cook for a minute.

- Add wine to deglaze the pan. Transfer pan mixture to the slow cooker.
- Add broth, vinegar, and herbs to the slow cooker.
- Cover slow cooker and cook on low for 8 hours.
- Serve and enjoy.

Nutritional Value (Amount per Serving):

- Calories 241
- Fat 13.4 g
- Carbohydrates 3.1 g
- Sugar 1.3 g
- Protein 20.4 g
- Cholesterol 53 mg

Roasted Pork Shoulder

Time: 9 hours 10 minutes

Serve: 8

Ingredients:

- 4 lbs pastured pork shoulder
- 1/2 cup water
- 1 tsp garlic powder
- 1/2 tsp ground black pepper
- 1/2 tsp sea salt

Directions:

- Season pork with garlic powder, pepper, and salt on all side and place in slow cooker.
- Add water and cover and cook on high for 1 hour then turn heat to low and cook for 8 hours.
- Remove meat from slow cooker and shred using a fork.
- Serve and enjoy.

Nutritional Value (Amount per Serving):

- Calories 664
- Fat 48.5 g
- Carbohydrates 0.3 g
- Sugar 0.1 g
- Protein 52.9 g
- Cholesterol 204 mg

Delicious Pork Chops

Time: 4 hours 10 minutes

Serve: 4

Ingredients:

- 4 organic pork chops
- 1 tsp dried basil
- 1 tsp dried oregano
- 1 tbsp poultry seasoning
- 1 tbsp garlic powder
- 2 garlic cloves, minced
- 1 cup organic chicken broth
- 1/4 cup olive oil
- Pepper
- Salt

Directions:

- In a large bowl, whisk together oil, basil, oregano, poultry seasoning, garlic powder, garlic, and broth.
- Pour bowl mixture into the slow cooker then place pork chops into the slow cooker.
- Cover slow cooker and cook on high for 4 hours.
- Serve and enjoy.

Nutritional Value (Amount per Serving):

- Calories 386
- Fat 32.9 g
- Carbohydrates 2.9 g

- Sugar 0.7 g
- Protein 19.7 g
- Cholesterol 69 mg

Healthy Lemon Dill Halibut

Time: 1 hour 35 minutes

Serve: 2

Ingredients:

- 12 oz wild Alaska seafood halibut
- 1 1/2 tsp dried dill
- 1 tbsp olive oil
- 1 tbsp fresh lemon juice
- Pepper
- Salt

Directions:

- Place halibut into the middle of large foil piece and season with pepper and salt.
- In a small bowl, whisk together lemon juice, dill, and olive oil.
- Drizzle bowl mixture over the halibut. Bring the edges of foil and crimp them together.
- Place the foil packet into the slow cooker and cook on high for 1 hour 30 minutes.
- Serve and enjoy.

Nutritional Value (Amount per Serving):

- Calories 470
- Fat 37.3 g
- Carbohydrates 0.6 g
- Sugar 0.2 g
- Protein 31.6 g

- Cholesterol 100 mg

Salmon With Carrots & Onions

Time: 8 hours 10 minutes

Serve: 4

Ingredients:

- 1 lb wild-caught salmon fillets
- 1/2 tsp dried dill
- 4 garlic cloves, minced
- 16 oz baby carrots
- 4 onions, chopped
- 2 tbsp olive oil
- 2 tbsp ghee
- 1/8 tsp pepper
- 1/2 tsp salt

Directions:

- Add ghee and olive oil in a slow cooker.
- Add garlic, baby carrots, and onions and stir well.
- Cover slow cooker and cook on low for 6 hours.
- Now place the salmon fillets over the vegetables in the slow cooker and sprinkle with dill, pepper, and salt.
- Cover again and cook on low for 1-2 hours.
- Serve and enjoy.

Nutritional Value (Amount per Serving):

- Calories 397
- Fat 23.6 g
- Carbohydrates 20.7 g

- Sugar 10.1 g
- Protein 26.1 g
- Cholesterol 86 mg

Cilantro Lime Salmon

Time: 2 hours 10 minutes

Serve: 4

Ingredients:

- 1 lb wild-caught salmon fillets
- 3 tbsp lime juice
- 2 garlic cloves, chopped
- 3/4 cup cilantro, chopped
- 1/4 tsp kosher salt
- 1 tbsp olive oil

Directions:

- Add olive oil into the slow cooker then place salmon fillets into the slow cooker.
- In a small bowl, combine together lime juice, garlic, cilantro, and oil.
- Pour bowl mixture over the salmon.
- Cover slow cooker and cook on low for 2 hours.
- Serve and enjoy.

Nutritional Value (Amount per Serving):

- Calories 228
- Fat 13.5 g
- Carbohydrates 1.4 g
- Sugar 0.2 g
- Protein 24.1 g
- Cholesterol 70 mg

Chicken With Artichokes

Time: 7 hours 10 minutes

Serve: 4

Ingredients:

- 2 lbs chicken, cut into pieces
- 4 garlic cloves, minced
- 1 lemon, sliced
- 1 onion, sliced
- 15 oz artichokes
- For sauce:
- 2 tsp thyme
- 1 tbsp olive oil
- 1/4 cup lemon juice
- 1/2 tsp pepper
- 2 tsp salt

Directions:

- Add onion into the slow cooker then add artichokes and chicken on top.
- In a small bowl, mix together all sauce ingredients and pour over chicken.
- Cover slow cooker and cook on low for 6-7 hours.
- Serve and enjoy.

Nutritional Value (Amount per Serving):

- Calories 444
- Fat 10.8 g

- Carbohydrates 15.5 g
- Sugar 2.6 g
- Protein 69.9 g
- Cholesterol 175 mg

Delicious Turkey With Gravy

Time: 6 hours 10 minutes

Serve: 8

Ingredients:

- 5 lbs pastured turkey breast
- 1 tbsp ghee
- 1 tbsp poultry seasoning
- 1 onion, sliced
- 1 tsp pepper
- 2 tsp salt
- For gravy:
- 1/2 tsp cumin
- 1/2 tsp pepper
- 1 garlic clove, minced
- 1/2 tsp Italian seasoning
- 2 cups organic chicken broth
- 1 tsp salt

Directions:

- Add onions, garlic, Italian seasoning, broth, cumin, pepper, and salt to the slow cooker. Stir well.
- Season turkey with poultry seasoning, pepper, and salt. Place season turkey into the slow cooker.
- Top with ghee. Cover slow cooker and cook on low for 6 hours.
- Serve and enjoy.

Nutritional Value (Amount per Serving):

- Calories 328
- Fat 6.8 g
- Carbohydrates 14.2 g
- Sugar 10.7 g
- Protein 49.9 g
- Cholesterol 126 mg

Delicious Beef With Mushrooms

Time: 6 hours 15 minutes

Serve: 6

Ingredients:

- 2 1/2 lbs grass-fed beef roast
- 1 tsp onion salt
- 1 tsp garlic powder
- 1 tbsp almond flour
- 1/2 cup organic chicken broth
- 1 tbsp olive oil
- 3 garlic cloves, minced
- 1 large onion, sliced
- 8 oz mushrooms, sliced
- Pepper
- Salt

Directions:

- Add onion into the slow cooker. Sprinkle roast with almond flour and season with onion salt, garlic powder, garlic, pepper, and salt.
- Heat olive oil in a large pan over high heat.
- Add roast to the pan and sear from all sides. Transfer roast into the slow cooker.
- Add broth and mushrooms over the roast.
- Cover slow cooker and cook on low for 6 hours.
- Shred the meat using a fork and stir well.

- Serve and enjoy.

Nutritional Value (Amount per Serving):
- Calories 230
- Fat 13.2 g
- Carbohydrates 4.8 g
- Sugar 1.9 g
- Protein 24.5 g
- Cholesterol 67 mg

www.ingramcontent.com/pod-product-compliance
Lightning Source LLC
Chambersburg PA
CBHW071440070526
44578CB00001B/165